No Way Out

No Way Out

Precarious Living in the Shadow of Poverty and Drug Dealing

WAVERLY DUCK

The University of Chicago Press
Chicago and London

Waverly Duck is assistant professor of sociology at the University of
Pittsburgh.

The University of Chicago Press, Chicago 60637
The University of Chicago Press, Ltd., London
© 2015 by The University of Chicago
All rights reserved. Published 2015.
Printed in the United States of America

24 23 22 21 20 19 18 17 16 15   1 2 3 4 5

ISBN-13: 978-0-226-29790-3 (cloth)
ISBN-13: 978-0-226-29806-1 (paper)
ISBN-13: 978-0-226-29823-8 (e-book)
DOI: 10.7208/chicago/9780226298238.001.0001

Library of Congress Cataloging-in-Publication Data
Duck, Waverly, author.
    No way out : precarious living in the shadow of poverty and drug
  dealing / Waverly Duck.
        pages cm
    Includes bibliographical references and index.
    ISBN 978-0-226-29790-3 (cloth: alkaline paper) — ISBN 978-0-226-
  29806-1 (paperback: alkaline paper) — ISBN 978-0-226-29823-8 (e-book)
    1. Drug traffic—Social aspects—Northeastern States. 2. Urban poor—
  Northeastern States—Social conditions. 3. Cities and towns—Northeastern
  States. 4. Sociology, Urban—Northeastern States. I. Title.
    HV4045.D83 2015
    305.896'073074—dc23   2015009522

♾ This paper meets the requirements of ANSI/NISO Z39.48-1992
(Permanence of Paper).

For Georgia, Anne, Charles, Eli, and Doug

CONTENTS

This book began when I was asked to collect ethnographic data about an impoverished black neighborhood to buttress an argument for mitigating circumstances in a federal death-penalty case. Although I grew up in a similar neighborhood, I was disturbed by what I saw transpiring in this community. Major social changes seemed to result from shifts in public policy, particularly welfare and housing reform, the war on drugs, and the rising costs of food, housing, and energy. I was puzzled about the interconnections among these factors and the community's embedded drug trade. At the same time, I was moved by the love, support, and solidarity that existed within the neighborhood. I am grateful to the countless residents, attorneys, journalists, activists, friends, and families who opened their homes and told me their stories, all of whom must remain anonymous.

In this community, the constraints are multiple, overlapping, and to an unfortunate extent mutually reinforcing: the absence of decent jobs and schools, the radical contraction of the social safety net, a criminal justice system that makes everything more insecure, and child-support laws that backfire on people with limited resources and job prospects. The few available economic opportunities carry real dangers. With no legal jobs nearby, you need to drive to work; but if you have been unable to pay traffic fines or car insurance, even minor traffic infractions can get you jailed. If you have no resources, managing child care and earning the income to support your family seriously impede each other. The multiple risks of the drug trade affect the whole community, not just users and sellers.

No Way Out: Precarious Living in the Shadow of Poverty and Drug Dealing is an homage to classic ethnographic and qualitative studies, especially W. E. B. Du Bois's *The Philadelphia Negro*, Joyce Ladner's *Tomorrow's Tomorrow*, Carol Stack's *All Our Kin*, Ruth Horowitz's *Honor and the American Dream*, Elliot

Liebow's *Tally's Corner*, Elijah Anderson's *A Place on the Corner*, Herbert Gans's *Urban Villagers*, Jay MacLeod's *Ain't No Makin It*, Gerald Suttles's *The Social Order of the Slum*, and Mary Pattillo's *Black on the Block*. It draws on the theoretical legacy of Emile Durkheim, Harold Garfinkel, Erving Goffman, and Anne Warfield Rawls.

A word about the title. The term "precarity" recently came into common usage in Europe, especially in the anti-globalization movement, to refer to the flexible, contingent, and casually employed labor force—which includes both low-wage workers in service positions and knowledge workers such as customer service representatives in technology companies' call centers. The best description of this global trend is Michael Hardt and Antonio Negri's *Multitude: War and Democracy in the Age of Empire* (2004). My usage, in contrast, focuses on the lives of my participants, rather than their labor: these people are, at best, employed only intermittently, and their entire existence, not just their income, is insecure. They are part of what used to be called the "underclass," rather than people whose well-founded expectations of financial security have been disappointed by neoliberal shifts in the labor market. The Catholic radical Dorothy Day once used "precarious" in the sense as I do here—to refer to the predicament of people living in chronic poverty.

No Way Out has been more than ten years in the making. No intellectual endeavor is possible without the support of friends, family, colleagues, and academic institutions. I would like to acknowledge Craig Alston, Nadine Amalfi, Elijah Anderson, Alan Artenstein, Dana Asbury, Ralph Bangs, Joyce Bell, Kathleen Blee, Scott Brooks, Rodd Brunson, Lisa Brush, Randall Collins, Megan Comfort, Andrea Cossu, Larry E. Davis, Ervin Dyer, Mustafa Emirbeyer, Mike Epitropolous, Anette Fasang, David Fasenfest, Myra Marx Ferree, Judith Gay, Robert Gay, Raymond Gunn, Keith Hagans, Jennifer Hamer, Juho Härkönen, Ruth Horowitz, Nikki Jones, Nancy Kasper, Ella Kemp, Esther Kim, Laurie Krivo, Charles Lemert, Peter Lichtenberg, Victor Lidz, Dwayne Lucky, Wynn Maloney, Peter Manning, John Markoff, Douglas Maynard, Reuben Miller, Dru Moorhouse, Peter Moskos, Joyce Oliver, Grey Osterud, Edward Park, Barry Pearlman, Anthony Peguero, Ruth Peterson, Anne Warfield Rawls, Barbara Ray, Victor Rios, Stevie Roberts, Suzanne Staggenborg, Lizzie Stoyle, Steven Swanson, Jason Turowitz, Randall Walsh, Loic Waquant, and Aaron Weller. To my mother, Georgia Duck, and my oldest brother, Maurice Duck, thank you for contributing to a moral compass situated in love and justice.

I am grateful to have received support from the University of Pittsburgh's Center on Race and Social Problems; Yale University, where I was a postdoctoral fellow while I conducted much of the fieldwork; and the students who changed my life at the Community College of Philadelphia, the Cheshire Twenty at the Cheshire Institutional Facility, and the University of Pittsburgh.

Finally, I owe special thanks to Doug Mitchell, who believed in this project from the beginning. His support has been unwavering and his friendship, invaluable.

What Ludwig Wittgenstein wrote in the introduction to his *Philosophical Investigations* captures my sentiments: "I should not like my writing to spare other people the trouble of thinking. But, if possible, to stimulate someone to thoughts of their own. I should like to produce a good book. This has not come about, but the time is past in which I could improve it."

Precarious Living

Although the United States has elected an African American president and the civil rights bill was passed more than fifty years ago, poor persons of color in many of our cities find themselves increasingly poor and racially isolated. On a street notorious for its thriving drug trade in an economically depressed and predominantly black city, I asked long-term residents how they felt about their neighborhood and why they stayed. Mrs. Wells, a seventy-eight-year-old African American, replied: "You know what, in a way it sounds crazy, but I feel protected. A lot [of] people who have moved out of the neighborhood have gotten broken in on, robbed. Here, I feel protected. As bad as it seems out there with the drugs and things, I feel protected. Because the guys out there with the drugs and things were out there doing their thing. They weren't going to break in on you and they weren't going to let no one else break in on you. Here I feel protected." That paradoxical response was typical rather than exceptional. In this community, the drug dealers are not outsiders but long-term residents who are well integrated into community life and protect it as their own.

Unlike the stereotypical image of drug-infested ghettos, this neighborhood is not plagued with crack houses and roaming addicts. Instead, its drug scene is controlled by a local group of young black men whose occupation is selling powdered cocaine to white suburbanites. While mostly black, the neighborhood residents are otherwise surprisingly diverse, including senior citizens, working-class families, longtime homeowners, African American Muslims, and even white Christian missionaries. I wondered: How do all of these people live together? How do residents make sense of the drug trade? How do both dealers and residents remain safe? What rules govern everyday life in this community?

First, we must ask why there is so much poverty and crime in this neighborhood. The answer I propose is rather simple. If people find themselves isolated in a place with no jobs, educational opportunities, or external social supports, they will organize for survival. A local cultural order, which I call an "interaction order" because it governs how people relate to one another, makes daily existence possible. This book, based on seven years of ethnographic observation and interviews, examines a neighborhood that I call Lyford Street in a small city in the northeastern United States that I call Bristol Hill (all places and persons are identified by pseudonyms). In this area, which has been in economic decline for as long as anyone can remember, it is nearly impossible for young black men to find legitimate employment, so drug dealing has become the principal occupation. The drug trade brings money from affluent white customers into this impoverished neighborhood and plays a vital role in the local circulation of resources. Rather than viewing drug dealing and the graffiti and occasional violence that accompany it as signs of disorder, I show that the local code of conduct that has developed around drug dealing is actually ordered in ways that shape the character of the entire neighborhood.

It is popular to consider the broken windows, trash, drugs, and graffiti that characterize such places as symptoms of disorder, a magnet for crime that is evidence of the community's failure to hold together and its lack of what Robert Sampson (2004) has termed "collective efficacy." To some outside observers, these sights even signify the absence of individual morality. But there was a great deal of personal responsibility and collective agency in the community I studied, and I suspect this may be generally the case. It only looks like disorder because it is geared toward survival in a context of isolation and exclusion from most of the opportunities that American society supposedly guarantees its citizens. The survival strategies adopted there do not resemble those familiar to the American mainstream.

Those who understand the difficulties of life in such neighborhoods often ask, Why don't people just leave? Most residents do not move away (Sharkey 2013). Within this enclave they have produced a form of life for themselves that they understand. There is no other place they understand as well or where they feel accepted. They have no way out. Generation after generation, they have organized for survival in the bleak and isolated spaces left to them as others fled and transformed impossible spaces into livable ones. Full and happy lives are lived under conditions that would make most Americans cringe. The point seems paradoxical, but it is important. These people do not want to be pitied. Instead, they ask to be treated with respect, like every other American with full legal rights. That they have been forced to live in such deprived places under the constant shadow of outside interference and legal jeopardy is a fundamental contradiction of the American dream.

The resourcefulness of generations in crafting a way of life under these conditions has come at a price. Alice Goffman's *On the Run* (2014) depicts the criminalization of entire neighborhoods by the surveillance state's "war on drugs." Residents live out their lives without access to jobs, attend failing schools that have been condemned by state boards of education, and often find themselves and their fathers, brothers, and sons imprisoned. The general public considers men in such places "scumbags" "gangbangers," and "thugs," in part because these terms are used on popular TV shows, and is all too willing to hold each individual accountable for the form of social organization in which they were raised. A typical posting to the website that supports the police officer who killed Michael Brown in Ferguson, Missouri, expresses the opinion that the shooting of this unarmed black youth was a "waste of good ammo. It's my privilege to buy you a replacement box." Another goes so far as to say, "I thank all Police . . . protecting normal Americans from aggressive and entitled primitive savages." These are not majority sentiments, but unfortunately they continue to have currency.

I argue that, contrary to popular misconceptions, conditions in such communities do not indicate a lack of social order or morality, but rather a highly developed social organization that enables people to survive under increasingly desperate circumstances. William Julius Wilson (1987) contends that the concentrated disadvantage has been intensified by the war on drugs, the criminalization of schoolchildren for minor offenses, the elimination of welfare programs, and the deterioration of schools. All this, combined with a lack of awareness on the part of many Americans that such conditions even exist, has forged profoundly isolated, oppressed, and volatile communities. Arguing against the common tendency to blame people in such places for being poor because they subscribe to a "culture of poverty," Wilson insisted that poverty, not culture, is the primary variable. In my study, I found that the culture of this place is directly responsive to the poverty and isolation against which people have organized for survival. Poverty is indeed a primary culprit. But so are the divisions of race and class that create the forces of isolation. The resulting local interaction order is a rational adaptation to otherwise impossible circumstances. It is an organization for survival in spite of overwhelming conditions; it is not an explanation of that condition.

While living under constant threat, the people I talked to have been successful at surviving, educating themselves and their children, and making money. But they have all had to do it in ways that violate the norms or laws of the larger society. Even families with good jobs must bend many expectations (legal and otherwise) to send their children to suburban schools and camps and avoid the many pitfalls of navigating between this place and the outside world (Gans 1995). The neighborhood remains their refuge. For them also there has been no way out. When asked why they stay, their appraisal of the benefits of staying in a community of known and familiar character is telling. They do not feel welcome or safe elsewhere. They know they are not safe here. But, like the others, they feel safer. So they stay.

Members of this community are living in a social order they understand. Even when they aspire to middle-class values, they recognize the origins of the local lifestyle in the need to survive and empathize with the young black men trapped here in lives of crime. Those men are also members of their community. When they look around them, they see vulnerable young men with few options (MacLeod 1987). That every member of this community understands the necessity of these survival strategies is an indictment of American society. Urban areas inhabited largely by impoverished African Americans and other marginalized people of color are typically imagined as chaotic places where drug dealing, street crime, and random violence make daily life dangerous for everyone. The physical dilapidation of rented housing, vacant storefronts, and empty lots reinforces the perception of social disorder that is assumed to characterize these neighborhoods. Many white Americans simply black out these places on their mental maps of the city and take care to avoid them. Policy makers, social workers, educators, and others concerned about those who live there have focused on identifying the sources of disorder in order to devise effective remedies for it. Approaching the problem as one of poverty and racial isolation would change policy dramatically. But such talk is not popular. What struck me most forcefully was that the local social order that is blamed for the problem by outsiders made residents like Mrs. Wells feel safe and even protected by the dealers who sold drugs to outsiders. This neighborhood's internal order ensured that no one broke into the homes of elderly people or mugged them on the street.

What the disorder approach overlooks is that social situations generate their own order, including rules that govern interpersonal interactions and make daily life relatively predictable. This ethnography explores the order that prevails in an impoverished black neighborhood with an embedded drug-dealing scene. Even events that appear senseless and chaotic from an outsider's perspective are seen by insiders as orderly and expected. Despite facing serious obstacles because of their race and their economic predicament, people in this neighborhood have generated a sustaining culture that contrasts sharply with the dominant culture. It is viewed with a toxic mix of incomprehension and hostility by outsiders. But to insiders it is home. I invite you to visit that place with me and see it through the eyes of its residents. They ask to be judged on their own terms—as human beings deserving of respect for the lives they have carved out amid impossible circumstances.

The Social Code of Lyford Street

Mastering the code of this street is a matter of life and death. In a neighborhood in which drug dealing is prevalent, residents must learn how the trade is organized in order to move through it safely. Most do not have cars, which means that going to school, to work, or to the store entails walking down streets where drug dealers are working. Residents must be able to interpret signs of trouble and, equally important, signal to drug dealers that they are not trouble: avoiding eye contact, not standing near dealers or their stashes of drugs and weapons, and not speaking unless spoken to. Most would, under other circumstances, be reluctant to interact with dealers. But in this community they have to engage them, whether passing them on the street, giving information to a dealer or to law enforcement, or warning their children about the dangers of involvement in the trade. Although most people who live in this neighborhood neither sell nor use drugs, they must pay careful attention to the routine activities of drug dealing and to the occasional incidents of violence that accompany it. In order to navigate their neighborhood, for example, even young children must be able to identify the boundaries of drug-dealing areas, recognize drug dealers, and know when they are working and exactly which job they are doing. A savvy child will assess the relative dangers posed by individual dealers and locations and take steps to avoid the more dangerous ones.

The code of the street, as initially defined by Elijah Anderson (2000), refers to the set of informal but commonly understood rules that govern interpersonal behavior in public when law enforcement and other formal means of settling conflicts are absent. In neighborhoods that are isolated from mainstream institutions and plagued by concentrated poverty and endemic unemployment, this code functions alongside the norms and values that residents call "decent," which most of them share with white, middle-class Americans. Learning to recognize what sort of behavior is appropriate to specific situations and to shift back and forth between "street" and "decent" modes of interaction is demanding but essential. Here I expand the concept of the code to encompass the entire set of interactions among residents and between themselves and outsiders on this street. In this setting, the most important distinction is not between "decent" and "street" behavior but between the values that residents share with most Americans and the local interaction-order properties of a place where drug dealing occurs.

Dealers' work practices and behavior in public spaces are well understood, and they get along peacefully with relatives, friends, and neighbors who are not involved in the trade. Indeed, during the years that I conducted fieldwork in the neighborhood, I was able to learn its ways well enough to observe drug dealing and other common legal and illegal activities, interview residents about most aspects of their lives, and socialize with people who were generous enough to serve as my guides—all without ever facing serious personal danger. The fact that I did volunteer work with children and families in nonprofit, church-sponsored programs helped; so did the fact that I first came to this neighborhood as part of the legal defense team for a young man falsely accused of murder. But the main thing that enabled me to explore this community for so long and in such depth was its own internal orderliness, an alternative set of rules governing personal interactions into which I gradually became initiated.

The practices that I observed in Bristol Hill are significantly different from those described in studies of impoverished black neighborhoods in major American cities, suggesting that smaller urban areas might have their own unique characteristics. The local social order constitutes a closely circumscribed context that has its own rationality and its own contours of time and space. People who lived in the neighborhood were closely linked by long-standing ties of kinship and friendship that knit them into an intricate social network. A person's identity was in part defined by his or her relationships with others, and no one could entirely sever these ties. Perhaps inner-city neighborhoods are less stable over time and less densely organized around enduring personal connections. Or maybe there are complex local orders that are largely overlooked. The local social order in the Bristol Hill neighborhood is fluid and has distinct temporal rhythms; a particular place may have characteristic practices at certain times and host quite different denizens and activities at others. Residents are attuned to these nuances, which makes the neighborhood comprehensible and enables security amid the flux and improvisation that living in poverty and isolation entails.

Trust, mutual understanding, and reciprocity form the bedrock of social organization in this community. The social obligations that exist between residents are essential to understanding how people navigate the neighborhood. In order to survive, everyone must become competent in the normally expected practices that constitute the situations they walk into and out of during the course of daily life, accurately interpreting what is going on there and responding in ways that others deem appropriate. Just as someone who wants to be a successful receptionist in a corporate office must become competent at greeting people and deciding who does and does not belong, people in this neighborhood must become competent in the practices that structure the events and interactions that compose everyday life. What underpins the interaction order in this community is a shared understanding of meanings that belongs to this space. As a known member of this community, a degree of reciprocity and mutual respect is expected, which contributes to the social solidarity of the neighborhood. The dealers may sell drugs to outsiders, but, most importantly, they are members of a community that requires of them a level of mutual reciprocity with regard to their family and friends.

The Local Interaction Order

Sociologists and anthropologists have used ethnography to make sense of communities on their own terms, especially their distinctive local cultures. The ways in which people's interactions produce order in impoverished black communities and the means by which residents who are differently positioned with regard to drug dealing adhere to that order are not well understood. This book illuminates how the local interaction order of this community shapes entry into drug dealing and how the presence of drug dealing shapes social interactions more broadly. To do so, I adopt an approach that brings the daily lives of insiders into focus and casts the local culture against the local challenges it must meet, correcting the distorted perceptions that outsiders tend to have of marginalized communities. An interaction order is a set of sense-making tools and strategies oriented toward the exigencies of a specific place (E. Goffman 1983; Rawls 1987, 2000, 2009; Fine 2003), in this case a neighborhood with an embedded drug scene as a principal source of work. The interactional practices I observed here comprise a shared context of background conditions (Garfinkel 1963, 1967; Rawls 2009) that shape how persons and actions are seen: what a particular gaze means, what a way of walking means, or whether a way of dressing is a threat or marks a trusted identity. More broadly, I explore how the drug trade affects everyone who lives near Lyford Street in Bristol Hill. This local interaction order is not about individual values and beliefs; it is how people organize to act and respond reflexively in a community where drug dealing is a principal occupation (Matza 1964).

A richly detailed understanding of the interaction order is exhibited in the account of a sixty-year-old black resident named Mr. Guthrie, who compared this neighborhood to a kingdom with a varied cast of actors who all have a particular role to play. His direct interactions with drug dealers are limited, but he acknowledges that they are his neighbors. This acknowledgment is reciprocal: as a recognized member of this community, he is known and protected. "See, we are safe here. We are safe. If I have a problem, then they're going to take care of it, 'cause I'm part of their kingdom. And I'm a big part of their kingdom. You know how safe that makes you feel? You know how it is to walk out your house and everybody speaks. Everybody speaks. I don't even know their names sometimes. You know, nine out of ten of these girls around here are Baby, Sweetie, Honey. You know, nine out of ten of these guys are Little Bro, Bro, Young Buck, whatever, you know. Don't even know their names. But they make you feel wanted, make you feel special. And you know what, I need them as much as they need me, 'cause they make me feel special. They really do, you know. It's wild. I'll do anything for them." The poor and racially oppressed have managed to create a context of mutual respect here that they experience nowhere else.

I want to emphasize that the culture of this community should be seen as an adaptation to isolation and poverty. It is not the cause, but rather the consequence, of racial isolation and poverty. This distinction is crucial. As Wilson insisted, if we do not recognize that the circumstances of poverty and isolation come first, then we end up blaming the victims of injustice as if they had created that injustice by having an inadequate culture. The interaction-order approach to cultural sociology examines culture as a way that ordinary people create order in everyday interactions. This common-sense approach to understanding and navigating the world provides insights into what every resident needs to do to navigate this space. Their culture is not inadequate. It is adequate for the place and challenges they face. To change the local culture would require first changing the circumstances of poverty and isolation.

This book explores those circumstances through residents' practices, first-person narrative accounts, and demographic information about the history of the Lyford Street community, which highlights the importance of policy changes with regard to housing, welfare reform, and policing. Several classic studies have focused on interaction in marginalized settings, most notably Gerald Suttles's *The Social Order of the Slum* (1966), Howard Becker's *Outsiders* (1973), and Lawrence Wieder's *Language and Social Reality: The Case of Telling the Convict Code* (1974). In exploring these places' internal social order, these studies highlighted how structural changes, such as the decline of manufacturing and rising unemployment, influenced residents' daily lives. I treat the combination of structural shifts and continuing patterns of racial discrimination as the context within which the local interaction order has emerged. On Lyford Street, the strong commitment of young adult men to the drug trade rests, to a significant degree, on their realistic understanding of the near-total absence of formal employment opportunities, the poor quality of the education available in their community, the low levels of property values and homeownership in the neighborhood, and their families' lack of savings and other assets. None of these factors has diminished their determination to support themselves and contribute to the support of those to whom they are bound by ties of kinship, friendship, and romance. Their moment-to-moment decisions about what to do and how to interact with others are guided by deeply embedded local social expectations.

Conversely, although young men's initial involvement in the drug trade may stem from familiarity with and proximity to drug dealing, their commitment to this career as adults is reinforced by their chronic inability to secure other livelihoods (Adler 1993; Murphy, Waldorf, and Reinarman 1990). Youths with arrest records are seldom hired for the few jobs that are available in the region, regardless of how long they have been law-abiding, and the stereotype of black criminality limits the job opportunities of all black men (Holzer and Reaser 2000; Pager 2008; Pettit and Western 2004; Western and Pettit 2000). Being aware that they face limited prospects for success in the dominant society affects whether young people take an interest in the future or focus on survival, pleasure, and success in the moment (Holzer, Offner, and Sorensen 2005).

The Lyford Street neighborhood exhibits the ordered properties of a relatively stable social situation. This order has a constitutive character—that is, it imposes requirements that shape what people do—and takes into account the complex interaction between residents and outsiders, such as social-service providers, property owners, law enforcement, and educators. This interaction order creates clear expectations (Garfinkel 1963, 1967) that all must observe; those who do not conform do so at their own risk. While drug dealing is a dangerous business, residents and frequent visitors take dealers' practices into account, and the dealers recognize these other actors as well. This order, which is ultimately based on reciprocity, is the fundamental source of safety.

Understanding the agreed-upon rules of this neighborhood as exhibited in residents' daily practices offers valuable insights into similar communities in other places, particularly the many small cities in economically depressed regions of the northeastern and midwestern United States. These social expectations order life events in predictable ways. Not only residents but drug dealers themselves can calculate the dangers they face and minimize the risks they run. In such places, the underground economy is an inescapable local social force. I do not mean to suggest that residents are victims of circumstance; rather, their actions and choices can be seen as intelligent and rational responses to their situation. They have refused to be willing victims. A better understanding of how residents order their lives in response to their environment can dispel stereotypical notions of "neighborhood decay" and "poor values" and point to more effective ways of improving the lives of people who struggle every day in such difficult surroundings.

Positioning Myself as an Ethnographer

Over the course of seven years of ethnographic fieldwork, I observed a local order that remained internally consistent, although it was periodically disrupted by events like shootings, stickups, and police interventions. My project was designed to incorporate a variety of perspectives over a range of places and times. To clarify what I did and did not do in Bristol Hill, several competing understandings of ethnography must be addressed.

According to those who have adopted the model originating in anthropology, a study is ethnographic only if the researcher moves into the area and lives with the people under study for an extended period of time. In the case of drug dealing, however, that approach would entail participating in dangerous and perhaps compromising activities. For a black man like me, that was not an option. More importantly, living in a community can narrow the observer's viewpoint in significant ways. The ethnographer may be forced to align him- or herself with one group more closely than others, narrowing and biasing his or her perspective. As an ethnographer, I chose not to live, work, or identify with the drug dealers I studied. It was important for me to remain neutral so that I could enter into many overlapping groups. Over time, most people got to know me primarily as a teacher and former social worker. I was forthright about my research, making it clear to everyone that I was there to study the neighborhood. My role as a researcher enabled me to get to know a wide range of people who live around Lyford Street. Like many ethnographers, such as Lois Presser in *Been a Heavy Life* (2008), Elliott Liebow in *Tally's Corner* (1967), and Elijah Anderson in *A Place on the Corner* (2003), I chose specific locations around which to focus the research. Although I developed relationships with hundreds of people in the neighborhood over the course of seven years, entering the area to observe drug-dealing activities was always dangerous—as it is for residents and for the dealers themselves. Unlike the drug trade in large cities, which takes place quite openly, the drug dealing conducted on Lyford Street is shrouded in secrecy and closed to outsiders.

Ironically, the best way to observe the full range of activities on Lyford Street was to remain in the role of an outsider who could be identified within the local interaction order and whose presence on the street was expected and normalized. I explained the goal of my research in discussions with neighborhood residents, realizing that drug dealers would soon get this information—and they quickly found ways to let me know they had heard what I was doing there. They checked me out in various ways. I adopted the public self-presentation of a social worker or social service provider walking in the neighborhood. Once I was accepted as a curious, somewhat helpful, but relatively non-intrusive outsider, I could observe the passing scene with relative freedom. Developing close relationships with several informants who had drug-dealing careers on the street deepened my understanding of the trade. But rather than focusing on drug dealing itself, I explored the ways in which the presence of drugs as a principal occupation and the local order practices it engendered shaped the local order of the neighborhood as a whole.

Neighborhood Solidarity

The popular media tend to depict drug dealing as a predatory activity, controlled by pushers and gangs who stand apart from the neighborhoods on which they prey. This may (or may not) be true in some large cities. On Lyford Street, however, drug dealers belong to the neighborhood and are integrated into the local community. Born and raised in the neighborhood, they are the brothers, sons, fathers, and cousins of those who are not involved in the trade. Not only do they contribute to the physical security and financial resources of others, but they also depend on social support from residents—not least their refusal to inform the police of illegal activities that do no harm to residents.

Drug dealers' integration into this neighborhood is even more complete than Sudhir Venkatesh (1997, 2006) found in Chicago, where residents and dealers had a cooperative relationship (see also Pattillo-McCoy 1999; Maher 1997). In big cities, dealers seldom live in the places where they work, and their anonymity contributes to their security; they can appear from nowhere and disappear just as suddenly. On Lyford Street, by contrast, their identities are well known. But their neighbors do not reduce them to their drug-dealing careers, understanding them instead in terms of their multidimensional connections with others. While many residents are overwhelmingly opposed to drug dealing, a significant number of them recognize that these young men resort to dealing because they have no other economic opportunities and are determined to be contributors rather than dependents. Ironically, they believe in American individualism and see themselves as entrepreneurs. Both dealers and non-dealers understand clearly that in such a small city, their street is one of only two viable locations for the trade. Indeed, Lyford Street has been the principal drug-dealing street in Bristol Hill for more than thirty years. Individuals move in and out of the trade, but the activity persists, and its practices are stable enough to be predictable.

Except for the aggressive police presence it provokes, the drug trade did little direct harm to the neighborhood. The primary commodity sold was powdered cocaine, not crack or heroin, and the dealers neither used the drug themselves nor sold it to local residents (marijuana was the drug of choice used by dealers). Typical markers of drug dealing such as boarded-up windows and broken streetlamps were indeed prevalent. An influential account by James Q. Wilson and George Kelling (1982) interprets broken windows as vandalism, memorial murals as graffiti, vacant lots as symptoms of neglect, and piles of trash as uncollected litter. This "broken windows" theory suggests that disorder and decay lead to further deterioration of the physical and social fabric of a neighborhood and open it up to predators. On Lyford Street, however, these features were carefully maintained; streetlamps were regularly shattered after city workers fixed them, as drug dealers paid others to plunge the street into darkness to enhance their security. Trash played a similarly strategic role.

During the mid-1960s, white outsiders and policy makers ascribed the problems that beset urban black communities to a "culture of poverty" that is allegedly inferior to that of the dominant middle class (Lewis 1961; Moynihan 1965; Mayer 1997). Residents were said to lack appropriate values and to live in a state of chaos, rather than being guided by social norms. The recent, less racialized formulation of this viewpoint centers on social disorganization as resulting from poverty (Small, Harding, and Lamont 2010; Harding 2010). Neighborhoods are often pictured as inviting the attention of drug dealers because they lack the collective efficacy necessary to remedy their pervasive physical and social deficits (Morenoff, Sampson, and Raudenbush 2001; St. Jean 2008). Collective efficacy, which Robert Sampson, Stephen Raudenbush, and Felton Earls (1997) define as "social cohesion among neighbors combined with their willingness to intervene on behalf of the common good," asserts that the people who live in this place lack social cohesion. According to these accounts, the force of collective efficacy could actually diminish crime rates in impoverished neighborhoods, because residents and criminals are seen as having opposing interests. Significantly, the articles that propagate these views sometimes quote drug dealers who disagree with the researchers and contest this interpretation of their actions (Jacobs, Topalli, and Wright 2003; Jacobs 2004; Jacobs and Wright 2006). From the dealers' perspective, the drug trade is less an opportunistic way of exploiting weak social links and more about generating livelihoods, fostering social cohesion, and maintaining a positive relationship with the neighborhood. On Lyford Street, social solidarity between drug dealers and other residents protected both the trade and the neighborhood. The classic type of collective-action attempt to improve social solidarity (collective efficacy), such as tearing down boarded-up houses and razing dilapidated playgrounds, instead resulted in increased neglect and disorder in the neighborhood, in contrast to what the "broken windows" theory predicts (Wilson and Kelling 1982).

Studies of drug dealing generally endorse the view held by law enforcement officers that the trade is organized and controlled by gangs (Short 1974). In large urban areas, it makes sense that dealers would be organized to reduce competition and evade police detection. In smaller urban areas, however, different strategies may be employed. The corporate type of criminal organization found in places like Chicago would not have the same utility in a small neighborhood. Although an organized structure obviously operates behind the supply and financing of the drugs sold on Lyford Street, the dealers themselves function as independent entrepreneurs with direct connections to suppliers. Typical elements of gang organization, including formal initiation processes and naming with an obligation to a single organization, are absent. Nor can dealers move frequently to avoid being identified. They have nowhere to go. Not only are individual dealers well known on Lyford Street, but many residents assured me that it is understood to be a requirement that they live or once lived there.

Loyalty to Place

The relationship between law-abiding citizens and drug dealers on Lyford Street runs very deep. Most dealers belong to families who have lived in the neighborhood for generations. Other family members may have legitimate employment and own their own homes. The dealers grow up, marry, and raise their children on the street where they work.

Unlike dealers in large cities, who may compete for the best places to sell drugs, the dealers on Lyford Street face a different challenge: to make the permanent space they occupy as secure as possible and defend it against encroachment by outsiders. As a consequence, drug dealers in Bristol Hill have a very strong attachment to place. In fact, a strong attachment to place characterizes the neighborhood as a whole. In my conversations with residents, I was surprised to find that few people would leave if they could afford to do so. At least four very successful families have elected to remain in the neighborhood because of the high value they place on local ties. I was told that insider status requires not only living in the neighborhood but also either being born there or having relatives who were. This definition of community membership is more typical of a village than a city; residency involves a level of collective solidarity not extended to outsiders.

Since dealers have worked the same spot for several decades, police knowledge of their activities is extensive. I learned from time spent doing fieldwork with the Bristol Hill police that they know a great deal about drug dealing on Lyford Street. I observed extensive undercover surveillance operations; these activities are quite obvious, such as working on electrical wires or streetlight poles for three weeks without accomplishing anything. The police do arrest dealers with some frequency. But any inference that inept police practices are responsible for the failure to curb drug dealing on the street overlooks essential aspects of this social context. The drug dealers on Lyford Street have developed sophisticated work practices that, combined with the benefits of location and neighborhood solidarity, make it difficult for the police to actually catch them with drugs. When they are caught, others, often family members, are ready to step in and continue the work. Residents who are not involved in the trade help to enforce the rule that only dealers who reside in the neighborhood can work on Lyford Street by informing police of the presence of outsiders. Local dealers use their knowledge of the space to target strangers for robberies.

Equally important, drugs are rarely sold from the family home. The corner is the default space. While I was working with the neighborhood patrol officer, I witnessed a resident who worked closely with the dealers pointing out people who tried selling drugs in their homes rather than the open air. This rule, like the residence requirement, is enforced through high levels of cooperation between residents and the police. Drug dealers realize that they cannot afford to jeopardize their families and friends, so they insulate them as much as possible from the risks that attend their illegal activities. In return, they enjoy the protection that this well-organized neighborhood can offer.

Drug dealers on Lyford Street are deeply enmeshed in extended kin networks. The drug-dealing network I knew the most about consisted of brothers, uncles, and first and second cousins, along with their closest friends. Within these tight connections among neighborhood insiders, the dealers absorb both economic and personal risk in the same way a small-business owner would. Their practices are aimed at protecting the spot where they work, avoiding arrest and, when they are detained, providing a replacement source of labor. Most of the men in this neighborhood cycle in and out of prison, and most of the children growing up here have fathers, brothers, uncles, cousins, and/or grandfathers in prison. Indeed, drug dealing and kin networks are so closely intertwined that making a distinction between them is difficult.

While the intimate relationships between dealers and non-dealers severely compromise the effectiveness of police intervention, the men in this neighborhood are in constant legal jeopardy. Federal, state, country, and local law enforcement agencies all have a heavy presence here, and arrests are made quite frequently. Yet the high number of arrests does not affect the availability of drugs. Nor does it change the fact that there is no other available occupation. For many residents, police intervention is an intrusion that creates chaos and danger, not order and protection. Since the early 1980s, this neighborhood and its residents have suffered from disproportionate contact with law enforcement agencies with no benefit to anyone. Children growing up in the neighborhood are exposed to the practices of both drug dealing and police action from an early age, and most get caught up in both the social order practices that facilitate and protect the work of drug dealing and the criminal justice system that sanctions them.

The extended kinship networks that link drug dealers on Lyford Street are not gang organizations. Defining them as a gang affords the police additional powers in dealing with them under the statutes designed for the prosecution of "racketeer influenced and corrupt organizations"—the RICO Act. But the best-informed police officers realize that the application of these laws to local drug dealers is a legal fiction. It is problematic to treat a kin group as a criminal conspiracy. Although the statutes were originally targeted at organized crime syndicates that intersected with kinship groups, they are supposed to apply only to organizations that are formed in order to pursue an illegal activity while avoiding legal consequences. Kinship groups are a natural social formation; whether or not some members pursue illegal activities, they have not been formed in order to do so. Furthermore, membership in a kinship group is not a matter of individual choice. Nor can an extended family network be broken up in the ways a criminal conspiracy can; it exists through the blood relations of the members. Above all, neighborhoods that are knit together by kinship ties and long-term affiliations have a strong basis for social solidarity and exhibit great resiliency in the face of external pressures.

The Disconnection between Values and Social Practices

The idea that poor urban neighborhoods are orderly places is not new. Since William Foote Whyte's *Street Corner Society* (1943), ethnographic studies have documented the orderly character of social interaction in settings inhabited by poor and racial-ethnic minority residents. The classic focus on culture as a set of shared values tends to treat features of social order as attached to people and groups and thus sees the visible order of drug dealing as the outcome of individual or group actions that are in accord with their beliefs, values, and goals, placing the emphasis on individual values. The focus on interaction order, however, inverts this relationship, placing the emphasis on the expectations and rules of a place rather than its people. The order is not a contingent and merely aggregate result of congeries of particular acts. Instead, it is a set of practices that enable mutually coordinated sense-making in specific places and situations. That is, it is a constitutive requirement of mutually intelligible action in that place.

Values and beliefs, as well as the traditional forms of social solidarity based on them, mean nothing until they are exhibited in actions that are understood by others. Local practices constitute the orderly and meaningful character of the public places and situations that people navigate in everyday life. Competency and trustworthiness in others' eyes are achieved through the situated practices in which people engage, not in the assumptions they make about others or the values and beliefs they may share. A person's gaze, walk, greeting styles, dress, and demeanor all convey information about his or her relationship to and status in the local interaction order. It is my position that in this neighborhood, the job requirements of drug dealing and their interface with the practices of residents and of law enforcement compose a local order in its own right. All participants in the situation must understand it in order for them to perform appropriately in that space. In this intersubjective arena, people must not simply conform to but proactively enact the local order if they are to fit in and be perceived by others as recognizable and accepted participants. Moreover, in dangerous urban spaces in which anomalies are predictably unpredictable, the need to present orderly and expected behavior is greater, not less, than in the more routinized spaces of suburban and middle-class urban life.

Let me be clear: a focus on beliefs, values, and norms as the foundation of social order can be seriously misleading. It fails to acknowledge both the yawning gap between people's intentions and their actions, which they often cover over with exculpatory rationalizations, and the many values and beliefs that people living in poverty share with the American middle class but are unable to achieve because of socioeconomic inequality (Young 2006). More fundamentally, it obscures the situated and constitutive character of the interactional practices that characterize specific social locations. The interaction order documented in this book is not a product of residents' values and beliefs, which are ironically quite conventional. It is, rather, generated through the concrete, intricately ordered practices they enact as they engage with one another and with the outsiders who frequent their neighborhood. Individualistic and group-level explanations do not work in this context. The residents of this neighborhood do not act purely as autonomous individuals; that would produce a level of chaos that is remarkably absent. At the same time, they do not form a group in the classic sense; they are not united by affiliations and traditions that mark them off from others. They are only a group in the sense defined by Harold Garfinkel and Anne Warfield Rawls (2006): they have committed themselves to a specific set of rules for organizing their interactional practices. For some residents, the local interaction order is all they have in common with others in their neighborhood. But for most, it is more than they can count on elsewhere.

Historically, black men in Bristol Hill have been excluded from opportunities for legitimate employment. If decent jobs were to materialize, this picture might quickly change. In a sense, drug-dealing careers are distorted imitations of the kinds of careers pursued by educated men from less disadvantaged backgrounds. But for decades now, drug dealing has been the only available means of earning a livelihood for these men. Like any other form of work, it creates a whole array of social positions: not only buyers, sellers, distributors, and producers but also rivals and police. All of these place constraints on the activities that occur in and around the drug trade. The ability to recognize and take effective action with regard to this complex organization is key both to successfully doing the work of drug dealing and to living in its midst. Everyone inhabiting this space must become competent in interpreting and performing these practices. The fact that drug dealing is an illegal activity that involves high financial and personal risks—such as bad loans to addicts, robbery by other dealers, and arrest—only increases its impact on the local interaction order.

Drug dealing does not constitute a norm of action for residents, nor is it a normatively valued activity. As Guthrie's description of this "kingdom" indicates, residents and drug dealers live together in mutually beneficial ways. Accepting and abiding by the interaction order of drug dealing is not a defense of drug dealing; it is simply an existential requirement of this neighborhood. The local practices that they enact tend to support the drug trade, even when it clashes with residents' own values. For instance, the prevalent reluctance to call the police about local dealers and the deference exhibited toward them amounts to collusion with crime by those who do not commit it themselves. At the same time, citizens of all classes tend to protect the privacy of their own families. Avoiding drug-related spaces and censuring relatives who become involved in the trade are consistent with middle-class values. Middle-class whites are also much less likely to report their drug-involved children to the police than to take them to psychiatrists, social workers, and treatment programs. The residents of this neighborhood are no different. Deeply committed to middle-class values, they lack the resources to fulfill them.

The niche occupied by impoverished black neighborhoods like Lyford Street is defined structurally by the absence of legitimate job opportunities for men. Long-term residents recognize the circumstances that make the drug trade the only means of livelihood available to young men. Mr. John, a sixty-seven-year-old long-term resident, is locally regarded as a success story because he is gainfully employed. Many dealers seek his advice for ways of finding a job in hopes of not returning to jail. He offered an eloquent, and deadly accurate, account of their predicament.

You read the paper about these guys out there selling the drugs and all that kind of stuff. And they're not all bad guys. Well, some of them are but most of them aren't. But when you belong to that world. . . . Now, like I said, I don't sell drugs, I don't do drugs, but I'm in a world with them, you know. This is their world. If I go down, guys on the corner could be selling drugs. There're a million out there. If I fall down in the middle of the street, that guy is going to come over to me to make sure I'm OK. And that's the hard part. No, I don't want to see 'em selling drugs. No, I definitely don't want to see 'em selling drugs. And if I can get by . . . if there was some kind of magic wand that I could take, I'd take it and none of them would sell drugs. And my magic wand would be to get rid of all people that took drugs, 'cause if you get rid of all people that take drugs, ain't no need for a person to sell drugs. But I also see the way the system runs. I've had people get felonies for selling drugs, and then they come over and knock on the door after they get out. I don't know why, but after they get out, they gotta come here and explain to me what happened. "Well, let me tell you, Mr. John, we don't want you mad." It's like, "Hey, it is what it is. Anything I can do." And I tell them the same thing: "Anything I can do, let me know." They say to me, "Well, do you know anybody hiring?" Then you go out there and look around and try and get them a job. And a lot of these temp places around here tell you, "Well, there is no jobs; he got a felony." Post office, if they got a felony, can't hire them. Then that same guy who just got out of jail two months ago, he has a family. It might not be a wife and the regular family, but he has kids or whatever. He needs a place to stay. What does he do? He goes right back to selling drugs. That hurts. That hurts.

Mr. John recognizes that the outside world in which he is gainfully employed has no room for former drug dealers. He also understands that he and the drug dealers have the sort of reciprocal relationship that creates mutual support. If anything were to happen to him, they would make sure he is OK. They would like his assistance, and it hurts him that he can do so little on their behalf. The dealers and residents who coexist in this space form a single community bound together by reciprocity.

The local order practices they share create a constitutive framework for social action, without which interactions and identities in this context would make no sense. In Erving Goffman's (1959) terms, they constitute performance criteria for establishing identity, competence, and loyalty in this place. As Harold Garfinkel (1967) argued, they both require and demonstrate mutual commitment and a high degree of reciprocity. Treating the practices characteristic of such places as an interaction order that requires a high degree of commitment and attention from residents challenges the prevailing understanding of poor black neighborhoods. The interaction order constitutes an important but overlooked form of collective efficacy, even though, forged as it is in a context of poverty and isolation, it often works against the visible expression of middle-class values. Because of the constitutive character of local interaction-order practices, it is a mistake to use standards that come from elsewhere to judge individuals who grow up there as if they were free to follow whatever rules they choose or to measure the solidarity and efficacy that characterizes these neighborhoods.

Until there is a way out, until jobs and education become available, and until the young men in such communities are treated by the police, media, and the general public as human beings of at least ordinary value, they will continue to organize for survival. The broader society may not like it, but one thing that history teaches is that the poor will not just roll over and die because it would be more convenient for the rich and powerful if they did so.

ONE

Jonathan's World

In 2005 I served as an expert witness in the legal defense of a drug dealer from Bristol Hill whom I call Jonathan Wilson. That project, which began with a limited purpose, turned into a long-term, in-depth ethnographic study as I became immersed in Jonathan's life, his family, and his community. I met Jonathan while he was in prison awaiting a death-penalty hearing after his conviction for being an accessory to the murder of a federal witness and murder of a rival drug dealer. The prosecution's main witness was the triggerman in the federal witness's murder. The murder charge was related to a cold case that had gone unsolved for several years. The defense team sought to show that the environment in which Jonathan had grown up mitigated the seriousness of his alleged crimes.

I started with a series of interviews intended to illuminate the circumstances that had shaped his life. Preliminary exploration led me to Jonathan's church; his elementary, middle, and high schools; the juvenile facility where he had previously been incarcerated; his family and friends; other drug dealers; and residents who either knew him or knew of him. As the research progressed, I talked with many people and became interested and involved in that community. Jonathan's account, supplemented by extensive ethnographic observation, raises serious questions about whether he and others like him are a danger to society—or whether society and its interests might be a danger to them.

My introduction to Lyford Street was organized by Jonathan's lawyer, whom I call Douglas. Douglas and a social worker took me to the neighborhood and pointed out various places of interest, including Jonathan's house. As we drove into the neighborhood from a nearby highway, the drug dealers were the first thing I saw; I found it astonishing that they were so noticeable. Equally amazing was that the drug trade I had heard about from the lawyers was still thriving: the same script with a different cast. The local drug culture was visible and distinctive. It had obviously played a role in Jonathan's life; it would shape the life chances of anyone who lived here. Moreover, the drug dealing that I witnessed was so obviously orderly that it, in effect, provided a template for the social interactions that prevailed in the whole neighborhood. The drug trade operated within a tight-knit community where familial and friendship ties were intact and residents shared a long history. I soon learned that people felt a fierce loyalty to the neighborhood, even if they could afford to move.

What I saw in this community immediately challenged both popular and expert notions of drug dealing as an agent of disorder, and I felt compelled to figure out what was going on. For the next seven years, I volunteered at two day camps, an after-school program, and a publicly funded community outreach program, and I worked as a community organizer at a neighborhood center. At the summer camp, I met the children who led me to Benita, the single mother whose story I tell at the end of this book. Participating in candlelight vigils for slain residents, I met locals who explained the killings in meticulous detail and recounted the interpersonal conflicts that had precipitated such violent acts. In fact, as residents discovered that I was doing this study, they would approach me, wanting to talk. A community-based police officer I met through my volunteer work was an invaluable resource in the early days of the research; through her I learned a great deal about the police perspective on the neighborhood. Over the course of my research, I talked with hundreds of Lyford Street residents both past and present, many of whom invited me into their homes. Some of them keep in contact with me to this day.

I had come to Bristol Hill through my work with Elijah Anderson at the University of Pennsylvania. A team of federal defense attorneys wanted to use Anderson's (2000) work on the "code of the street" to argue for mitigating circumstances in serious criminal cases, and he had asked me to give a talk to the group based on ethnographic data. After visiting the neighborhood, my next task was to meet with Jonathan in prison. Initially, it was supposed to be a onetime interview so Todd, Douglas's co-counsel, and I could tell his story at the conference. It sounded simple enough, but the process was complex. First, I had to wait a month for my background check to return. Then, when I tried to visit, the prison was on lockdown. On the next attempt, my paperwork was missing, which required an additional background check. Finally, once I had again been cleared, I had to wait another month to see Jonathan because I had to coordinate the visit to accommodate his co-counsel.

During this process, I learned the basics of Jonathan's case and discovered that he was severely depressed, knowing there was a real chance he would be put to death. Douglas informed me that Jonathan seemed to have shut down; he had stopped talking and gave primarily yes and no answers to questions asked by his counsel and by expert witnesses. Both attorneys were worried that he was sabotaging his case. Although I had reservations about participating in what seemed like a futile defense, I went ahead with our first meeting.

Visiting Jonathan

Getting in to see Jonathan meant going through three checkpoints: the lobby metal detector; a secure waiting room with portraits of the president, the warden, and the attorney general; and a hand scanner and another long inspection. The first meeting was largely a preliminary strategy session to determine whether Jonathan's life story would fit into the framework Anderson had projected. Given that the prosecution was seeking the death penalty, the question was whether Anderson's (2000) analysis of the code of the street could be used to explain Jonathan's choices as the product of his social situation.

I was initially struck by Jonathan's youth. Even though he was twenty-four at the time, six feet two and wearing a military green jumpsuit, he looked like a teenager. He made it clear that he was not interested in having visitors. When introduced, he said hello, but when I attempted to shake his hand, he acted as if he didn't see the gesture and sat down. Douglas's co-counsel, Todd, told Jonathan that I was there to get a few facts about his life so that I could present his story to a group of federal defense attorneys, who might serve as a kind of testing ground for the defense strategy.

After that introduction there were a few comedic moments. To break the ice, Todd began to draw on pieces of information from his initial meeting with me. He awkwardly pointed out the rather stereotypical similarities between Jonathan and me: "You guys have a lot in common. Waverly grew up in a poor neighborhood; you grew up in a poor neighborhood. He's a young black man; you're a young black man. He has tattoos; you have tattoos. He's a college professor; you want to be a lawyer." I couldn't help but laugh, which made Jonathan laugh, too. Picking up on this, I began to use humor to pave the way toward conversation. First, I told him that it had taken three months of trying before I was finally able to talk to him. I made light of the bureaucracy in prisons, from the lost paperwork and multiple checkpoints to the series of lockdowns.

When Jonathan started to relax, I asked him whether he was OK and told him I had heard that he was depressed. He responded by telling me that he was going through a lot and hadn't seen his mother in more than four months. I had met his mother in the parking lot a few weeks previously, after a failed attempt to see Jonathan. She had been admitted, but he had refused to see her. Jonathan even told his mother to stop visiting him altogether after she became upset when he told her that she was partially to blame for his troubles because she had moved out and left him behind when he was young. Jonathan also informed me that he had turned himself in to the police after they threatened to charge his mother with drug possession when they found a bag of cocaine that he had hidden in the house years before. In other words, he had sacrificed himself for her, but she was still unwilling to accept any responsibility for his situation.

Even more stressful was his wife's accusation that he was cheating on her with a former girlfriend, with whom he had a child. "Given that they're seeking the death penalty and your parents aren't cooperating, and you're in a maximum-security prison," I said sarcastically, "it doesn't make any sense that you would be cheating. Why does your wife think that? Where is this place where you're supposed to have this alone time with this other woman? So what's your secret? Because unless you're a magician, how is it possible for you to cheat with another woman in a maximum-security federal prison?" At that point his face relaxed and he said, "Thank you," as I was acknowledging if not completely understanding his chaotic life and current predicament.

Jonathan gave me basic information and later provided additional details about his neighborhood and how he became involved in drug dealing, at least enough for my presentation to the lawyers. He also began to trust me. In some ways, we did have a lot in common. We both got tattoos at fifteen to piss off our parents. We even had similar designs, including crosses to memorialize lost relatives and friends. Todd's awkward but well-intentioned attempt to get us talking worked, and eventually we became friends. When the first meeting was over, Jonathan not only shook my hand but also gave me a hug. In my mind, this was to be my one and only visit. Strangely enough, Douglas had other plans for me.

Presenting Jonathan's Life

Believing that my presentation to the attorneys was going to be my only involvement in Jonathan's case, I was extremely relaxed. I started with a PowerPoint presentation on *The Code of the Street* and then told Jonathan's story of getting involved in the drug trade, showing how his life was representative of the dichotomy between street and decent behavior portrayed in Anderson's book. I described Jonathan's family. Although his parents had separated and he was currently estranged from his mother, he grew up in a two-parent home, and both of his parents had been employed and owned their own home throughout his childhood. His family background almost seemed middle class, yet the drug trade embedded in his neighborhood snared him. I pointed out that sociologists have used frameworks such as human ecology and interactions with the lived environment to contextualize Jonathan's situation: his choices were only as good as his options.

After the presentation was over, the lead attorney, Douglas, invited me to dinner and asked a personal favor: Would I work on this case with him? Would I collect ethnographic information and ultimately testify on behalf of Jonathan? My first response was to say no, because I had no particular interest in crime or deviance and I barely knew Jonathan. Douglas did not take no for an answer, however. He explained that while he would value my research and input, he wanted me to testify because I was charming, likable, young, black, and well educated. He felt the jury needed to see me; they would respond positively, as had the audience at the conference. I was what Jonathan could have been had his circumstances been different.

When pressed, Douglas said: "Todd told me that Jonathan opened up to you during your meeting. He's been unresponsive with most of his visitors. But it's not only him; I think his family would talk to you as well. You have a way about you that makes people feel at ease. I barely know you, and I feel comfortable around you. You seem like a nice, likable, happy guy. You're good on paper and in person. The jury needs to know that not all young black men are drug dealers. If you tell his story the way you told it today, they may feel compelled to spare his life."

I agreed to testify on a voluntary basis. In fact, I spent a year and a half preparing for trial. Before I could testify, however, I had to be qualified as an expert witness. Having earned a Ph.D. in a relevant field was not good enough. When the case finally came to trial, the prosecutor argued that I didn't "deserve to be a witness" because I had "no courtroom experience" and "being a sociologist" did not "qualify" me as an expert. I pointed out that those statements were untrue; I had previously testified in family court as a social worker. Embarrassed, the prosecutor said, "Well, you never know these days, because he looks so young." The atmosphere in the courtroom was unpleasant, but I was determined to testify on Jonathan's behalf.

Divergent Paths

Jonathan's story resonated with me deeply because I had grown up on Detroit's East Side. My family had migrated to Detroit for better job opportunities in the auto industry. I was the first of my seven siblings born in Detroit. My family included a network of friends and relatives from rural Mississippi. As a child I had a tendency to get lost, often a few blocks away from home. On numerous occasions, our neighbors were able to study my face, figure out who my parents and siblings were, and take me home.

In the summer of 1983, the son of a neighbor and family friend, Percy, became the first crack dealer in my neighborhood. Percy's rise as a neighborhood folk hero was helped by the economic downturn the previous year, which led to layoffs for my father and many other men employed in manufacturing. Percy was among the new crop of black men in their late twenties and early thirties who were finding out just how lucrative the drug trade was. He had the money, the clothes, and a Mercedes—quite different from the older generation who preferred Cadillacs and Lincolns. Percy hosted a Fourth of July block party, financing most of the food and fireworks for the kids and creating a much-needed celebration in our economically depressed neighborhood. Although I was not aware of it at the time, the party signaled the transformation of my neighborhood. By October, a new phenomenon had made its appearance: crack addiction. Not one family was immune to the epidemic. I witnessed this problem firsthand with several relatives. Close friends and family members became almost unrecognizable. Formerly respectable men and women, now out of work, succumbed to the enticement of drugs, abandoned their children, stole to supply their habit, and were caught up in waves of violence because of competition among dealers and raids from the police. My family moved to the outskirts of the city when I was eight. But in less than five years, these problems had found their way into our new community as well.

My early teen years were shaped by the decline, death, and destruction of urban neighborhoods. In third grade when we relocated, I found myself in a diverse working-class space; Polish, Italian, Yemini, Saudi Arabian, and Hmong families surrounded us. We were the first of four black families on our block. By the time I got to middle school, however, the nonblack population had plummeted. Soon working-class and lower-middle-class blacks joined the exodus. When we relocated, the local high school had the second-largest student body in the city, with more than two thousand freshmen. Just 236 students graduated. But I left home during the eleventh grade because of the violence and economic deprivation that surrounded me.

At the age of seventeen, I moved to a small efficiency apartment in the Indian Village section of Detroit and worked two jobs, one as a box-office attendant at a local movie theater and the other as a janitor at an office building on the weekends. My stepfather, although separated from my mother, cosigned for the apartment, which helped to persuade a landlord who, despite his sympathy with my desire to escape a dead-end situation, was initially hesitant to rent to me. Those two years were the best of my teen life. Not only did I graduate from high school, but I saved enough money to pay for my first year of college ($5,000). But when I received a full scholarship to Connecticut College, I gave the money to my mother for the down payment on a new house, where she still lives to this day.

Bristol Hill was recognizable, almost familiar to me, because it, too, had gone through great transitions in its racial-ethnic and class makeup. Here, too, the only people who succeeded in avoiding involvement in drugs and crime were those who limited their interactions with others in the neighborhood. But this community was smaller, and some lower-middle- and working-class families remained, especially the first black people who had integrated the neighborhood in the 1960s. There were also a few white residents, mostly Christian missionaries from an organization that set up churches in poor urban spaces. The violence, although present, was not all related to the drug trade. Most important, in this community many familial networks were still intact. Lyford Street in Bristol Hill was resilient in ways that my neighborhood in Detroit had not been.

Jonathan's Family

Jonathan's parents described themselves as middle class, and they tried hard to maintain a middle-class existence despite their environment. Members of their church also described them in this way, making a distinction between the parents and their sons. When I told church leaders that I had worked on Jonathon's legal case, they spoke very highly of Jonathan's mother, describing her as a regular church member and an extremely religious woman. In an effort to protect their daughter, his parents sent her to a private school. But they underestimated the effects that marital conflict and the neighborhood had on their sons.

Jonathan's mother, Lynn Wilson, an African American, was in her early fifties when we first met. Winston Wilson, his father, was a Jamaican immigrant in his early sixties. I spent several hours with both parents listening to their accounts of how Jonathan became a drug dealer. Lynn also described how she met Winston. They married when they were in their late twenties, began having children, and purchased a house together on Lyford Street. Jonathan's sister, Nicole, was three years older, and his brother, Antonio, was two years older. Jonathan knew that his mother was originally from Georgia but grew up in Bristol Hill and that his father was from Jamaica. He had no contact with any of his grandparents, who had died when he was very young.

The home that his parents owned anchored them to the neighborhood, despite the drug dealing all around them. Both Lynn and Winston worked in Bristol Hill, Lynn as a nurse's aide and Winston as a security guard at the shipyard. Previously, Winston had worked at a factory until it closed in 1999 and then was unemployed for several years. Although they managed to keep their heads above water financially, it was not easy. The mortgage, private school tuition, and other expenses often strained their relationship, and they argued frequently about finances. Jonathan said that wanting and having money became very important to him because of these conflicts.

Lynn and Winston's marriage ended because of his infidelity. When Antonio was a baby, Lynn's best friend, Tina, needed a place to live and the Wilsons decided to take her in to their home. Tina, who had been Nicole's babysitter before she moved in, continued in that role and also took care of Antonio. Then when Lynn became pregnant with Jonathan, Tina had a daughter, Vanessa. Lynn had never met the father of Tina's baby and suspected that it might be Winston, but Winston denied having an intimate relationship with Tina. Tina moved out a few years later, but continued to babysit the Wilson children for several more years.

Eventually Lynn learned the truth. Jonathan was eleven when the revelation surfaced that Winston had fathered not only Tina's first child but also her two subsequent children. Although Lynn also learned that Winston had been providing financial support, he continued to deny that the children were his. He only admitted to fathering them when he testified at Jonathan's trial.

A Mother's Burden

Even before meeting Lynn, I realized that this entire experience was deeply troubling for her. I had heard Jonathan's side of the story; he held his mother partially responsible for his entry into the drug trade because she had left the family home (moving two miles away) when he was eleven. I realized that the actual situation was more ambiguous. Jonathan admitted that he and his older brother were involved in the drug trade long before his parents' separation and that they had used elaborate tactics to keep them in the dark about their skipping school and dealing. I knew from Jonathan's attorneys that Lynn did not want to testify at her son's trial because she was afraid for herself as well as for him. That reaction was understandable: she had been threatened with arrest by the truant officer for not sending her sons to school, and federal investigators had threatened to send her to jail for felonious possession of a firearm and drug possession after they found her father's World War II pistol and a small bag of cocaine residue hidden in a light fixture in her sons' room. She was also troubled that federal prosecutors in the same conspiracy case were seeking the death penalty for her older son, who had been diagnosed with an intellectual impairment in grade school. Antonio's low IQ ultimately enabled him to escape the death penalty, but he was sentenced to life in prison. Since Jonathan blamed Lynn for the family's woes, it was important for me not only to empathize and acknowledge what she had been through but also to get her side of the story. I was puzzled by the fact that Lynn's departure from the family home seemed to have affected Jonathan more deeply than his father's cheating, although her position as the head of the household, at least in her children's eyes, may have increased their distress.

During a chance encounter in the prison parking lot, I asked her to speak with me about her son's case. I was impressed by her appearance, which suggested a degree of self-respect that did not comport with the conventional image of a wronged wife. Lynn was a tall, very shapely, fair-skinned African American woman with high cheekbones and platinum blond hair that faded into its natural light-brown color. I began by explaining that everything that I knew about her was based on Jonathan's and the lawyers' reports and I wanted to hear directly from her. Our dialogue began somewhat awkwardly, but Lynn agreed to meet two days later.

I showed up at her home with a peace lily houseplant for her and a football for her nephew, a gesture intended to show that I appreciated her agreeing to talk with me. Her two-bedroom apartment was immaculate. Although it had tan wall-to-wall carpeting, Lynn had placed an area rug with gold borders in the living room. A matching gray plush sofa, chair, and loveseat were accented by deep purple and burgundy pillows. A square glass coffee table was positioned precisely in the middle. The furniture looked new; perhaps this room was rarely was used. After I gave her the gifts, we sat in the kitchen at a tall glass table in leather-upholstered swivel chairs. Giving her a hug like the one her son had given me, I thanked her for speaking with me.

"I warned them," Lynn began. "I told them if they get arrested I wasn't going to be there for them. They were on their own. They knew not to bring that stuff into my house. When I found drugs in his room, it was me who called the police; that is how he ended up on probation." Nonetheless, he was incredulous about the police allegations. "I don't believe anything they're saying about them being a drug gang with millions of dollars. Where is the money? He's poor, his wife's poor, his children are poor. The car is old and beat-up; he bought [it] for six hundred dollars. He was still borrowing money from me two weeks before he got arrested." She then acknowledged an important fact: "The only reason he turned himself in was because they were trying to charge me with felony firearm and drug possession."

I knew that Lynn had moved out of the family home for two years, come back for a shorter time, and then moved out permanently. After she alluded matter-of-factly to those events, I inquired, "What made you leave in the first place?" "I couldn't deal with the lies," she replied. "My husband was constantly lying to me, my sons were skipping and getting kicked out of school, my daughter changed schools then got pregnant, then the cheating. I couldn't take it. I suspected that he had cheated with Tina, but when her kids showed up to my house to see my daughter, I couldn't take it. She was my best friend, we were bumping bellies. Although I suspected [that Tina was sleeping with Winston], I was never sure." Her voice began to shake; her eyes welled up with tears as she recounted her struggles. "The debt, the stress, then Winston and I weren't getting along—I had to go. I tried going back, but I couldn't. All of the decision fell upon my shoulders. They were killing me. Everyone was deceiving me. I had to go. The situation speaks for itself. After I left I was in and out of the hospital for two years. I had to take care of my health. I was really sick; I'm still sick." After a moment's silence, I asked gently, "Do you want to talk about it, what was wrong?" "No, I don't want to talk about it," she said, "but when I was in the hospital it was serious. I don't want to talk about it." In response to my careful questions about how she was doing now, she acknowledged that she was taking an antidepressant and a sleep aid but avoided giving any details, at one point attributing her physical ills to "lady problems."

Refocusing our conversation on the family's problems rather than on Lynn's difficulties in dealing with them, I learned that before her final departure Jonathan had dropped out of school and been arrested twice for dealing drugs. She was also unable to control Nicole, who left private school so she could attend public school with her friends. Nicole became pregnant at sixteen. As far as Lynn could tell, Winston was continuing his affair with Tina. In order to save herself, she felt compelled to leave.

Jonathan's parents remained married, although they live separately. Lynn refused to divorce Winston mainly for financial reasons; they were joint owners of the house, and a divorce would entail legal fees. I also sensed hints of residual feelings for each other. For his part, Winston refused to move because of the investment in the house, and he anticipated that the state might purchase and demolish a number of the homes in their neighborhood for a redevelopment project.

I was struck by the fact that although throughout his court case Jonathan blamed his mother's abandonment for his entry into the drug trade, he did not know why she had left home. He speculated that it was because of his involvement in the drug trade and his sister's pregnancy, but it never occurred to him to consider his father's infidelity. He also did not take into account his mother's inability to maintain the quality of life that she worked so hard for. Jonathan never asked, and Lynn didn't volunteer her reasons to her son. This lack of communication only perpetuated the estrangement between them, which was as powerful as their mutual attachment was deep.

Becoming a Drug Dealer

Jonathan's story illustrates a path that many young boys in the neighborhood followed into drug dealing. (This same process likely occurs in other neighborhoods as well; see Black 2009; Moskos 2008; Sampson and Laub 1990, 1992). Jonathan began as a lookout at age eight, became a drug holder at eleven, and was a full-time drug seller on the corner at fourteen. Consistent contact with familiar neighborhood dealers facilitated this progression. Because of frequent arrests and even murder, turnover among drug dealers is high. Replacements are recruited from the young boys in the neighborhood. Older men exploit boys' strong family and friendship ties and promise them an income that seems substantial. Although most dealers I spoke with were well aware of the risks of death and jail time, they said that the prospect of steady money outweighed them.

Jonathan's first association with drug dealing came by earning small sums for doing errands at the store for a dealer. Many of the younger children compete for this task because they are allowed to keep the change. Sometimes Jonathan would also act as a lookout for law enforcement and/or potential customers. Three or four dealers at a time would work the block. Although a child might know all of the dealers and occasionally run errands for any of them, young boys were associated with a single dealer. Interviews with dealers, my observations, and a patrol officer's accounts corroborated the existence of an intricate network of dealers with very distinct roles. The networks are visible to anyone who lives there, and residents must learn to negotiate the daily interactions. Learning to walk in a way that says "you can ignore me, I am not a threat" becomes a survival skill.

Although not all the children in this neighborhood become errand boys, those who are unsupervised by their parents and come from families that are struggling financially tend to become involved in drug dealing. Most are initiated into drug dealing by male relatives or by familiar male members of the community. Residents know dealers as neighbors, relatives, and friends. In fact, the neighborhood is so closely knit that the families who manage to avoid drug dealing do so by making sure their children have no contact with other neighborhood children. They may send them to school in other towns so that both their sons and their daughters are on the periphery of local friendship networks. Accounting for these circumstances and understanding how they are shaped by the interaction order of an embedded drug scene sheds light on the recruitment process of vulnerable children. Relationships in the community are organized internally to make participation in the drug scene almost compulsory.

Jonathan's indoctrination into the drug trade began when a dealer being chased by the police thrust drugs into his hands and told him to "keep walking." When he tried to seek a safe haven by walking onto a neighbor's porch, the neighbor yelled at him, drawing the police's attention and resulting in his immediate arrest. By living in this neighborhood, Jonathan not only knew the drug dealer personally but understood that the cost of failing to comply with the dealer's orders could have included being subsequently attacked by peers who were also under the drug dealer's influence, being blacklisted so that none of the neighborhood kids would be allowed to talk or play with him, or suffering more direct physical punishment from one or more of the dealers themselves.

By the age of eight, Jonathan knew the informal code very well. During questioning at the police station, he continued to deny that the drugs were his and said that he did not remember the dealer who had given him the drugs. When his mother came to the station, Jonathan told her a partial truth: that he had been forced to hold the package. The lie was that he did not remember who had given it to him. In reality, he had known the dealer since he was six. Upon Jonathan's return, the dealers all talked about how much "heart" and courage he had shown by keeping quiet. His homecoming was celebrated, and as a reward for keeping the code, Dirty James, the twenty-three-year-old dealer he had helped, gave Jonathan forty dollars' worth of powdered cocaine to sell. Jonathan then made his first highly profitable drug sale. Jonathan's level of sophistication about his options in a situation with potentially serious consequences was informed by growing up on Lyford Street. Although Jonathan's mother had tried to teach him how to limit his interactions with local dealers, she was not surprised when he was forced to hold a package. She was all too familiar with the interaction order in this community.

Perhaps most important about Jonathan's first arrest is that he had virtually no choice as to whether to hold the drugs. In essence, Jonathan was in a double bind: he would inevitably be punished, either by the police or by the dealers. It is not obvious which choice is the more rational option (Duck and Rawls 2012). Neighborhood adults recognize this fact. According to Jonathan's mother, drug dealers use children as holders because "kiddie time" in juvenile detention is less damaging than "adult time" in jail. Although parents living in the neighborhood understand that this situation is detrimental to their children, they feel there is nothing they can do. Everyone seems caught in the web.

For almost all of these boys, the first arrest is the beginning of a downhill trajectory into a life of crime. Their involvement does not simply result from compulsion, however; the young men who deal drugs are also attractive models of manly success. The drug trade was alluring to Jonathan and other boys in the neighborhood because there were few other options for making a livelihood. High school was a place with a greater potential for violence than for useful learning, as fights occurred between youths from different neighborhoods in Bristol Hill. Attending school also interfered with Jonathan's ability to make money. When his mother left home, he was under much less surveillance, because his father simply paid no attention. To keep the news from reaching his mother, Jonathan intercepted truancy notices. It took a year and half before Lynn found out that Jonathan had dropped out of school. Fearing legal prosecution for allowing her son to be truant, Lynn reluctantly agreed to let Jonathan drop out of school permanently at sixteen. In fact, none of Winston and Lynn's three children finished high school.

There were two instances in which Jonathan tried to turn his life around. When his mother returned home briefly, Jonathan tried to change by leaving the drug trade and ceasing to use marijuana, but he still blamed his mother for abandoning him. The second occurred at age seventeen, when he was sentenced to probation that required random drug screening. After attempting to mask his urine with over-the-counter medication, Jonathan was hospitalized for drug poisoning. He stopped using drugs for a time. He was assigned a probation officer named Claire, whom he found sincere and caring. Claire arranged for him to take his General Educational Development (GED) test so he could qualify for jobs. She stopped by his home for visits, went to court dates, and kept up with his activities.

During this period Jonathan became the father of his first child. Although he did not marry his girlfriend, Susanna, he took his parental obligations seriously at first. As Jamie Fader (2013) and Jennifer Hamer (2001) have shown, fatherhood can contribute both to "going straight" and to an eventual return to dealing. A combination of pressure from Susanna and his own desire to provide for their child led Jonathan back to the drug trade. He and Susanna had been living off his savings, which he had been accumulating since he was fifteen. When the money ran out, one of Susanna's relatives fronted Jonathan the cash to start dealing again. At the age of eighteen Jonathan was caught, convicted, and sentenced to probation, but this time as an adult. He was assigned to another district, and Claire lost track of him.

At that point, Jonathan decided to look for legitimate employment. He interviewed for a job at a plumbing company. He had never even applied for a job, let alone held one. After struggling through the application and interview process, he was offered the job. Before he could start work, however, he had to present a valid government ID, which he did not have. The employer agreed to hold the job for a month while he got the ID. But getting a state ID and a Social Security card required a birth certificate. Although he asked his mother repeatedly, she failed to produce it. Apparently he did not know how to get a copy for himself. Philippe Bourgois (1995) and other researchers have found that many drug dealers are unprepared for the job market and do not understand what is expected, although many of the necessary skills can easily be taught. With few people in the community serving as role models or providing the needed information, the task of dealing with bureaucracy and even finding the right office can be insuperably difficult.

When I talked to Jonathan, he blamed his parents and run-ins with the law for his ignorance. "They never told me about how to fill out a job application, or even that I needed an ID," he said. In the meantime, while the plumbing company held the job for him, Jonathan and his brother continued to sell drugs. Jonathan used the profits to support not only his child but also his unemployed father and other family members, who accepted the money without question while openly condemning where it came from.

Cross-Examination

During the cross-examination at Jonathan's trial, the prosecutor asked me angrily, "Mr. Duck, isn't it true that his family was a decent family, that his mother was hardworking, that his father was hardworking, that these were good, decent people?" My response was that if decency is refusing to testify in your son's death-penalty hearing, if decency is abandoning your child so that he turns to drug dealing, if decency is having extramarital affairs and never admitting to them, then, yes, I guess these are decent people. That was the end of my testimony, and it changed the dynamics in Jonathan's favor in the courtroom. My response was cruel and judgmental. It exploited every aspect of shame and regret that Jonathan and his family had experienced throughout their lives. My intent was to discredit the prosecutor; in doing so, I insulted a family who truly did their best to survive given their circumstances.

Later, after doing much more fieldwork, I would have pointed out that four families on the street had managed to raise their children without contact with the drug scene. They did not do this by being "decent," however. Rather, they had the resources to keep their children off of the street. These children never played in the neighborhood and had no close friends there. They were sent to schools in another town. Their families had cars, so they did not even have to walk down the street. This lifestyle was expensive. It did not matter what the families' values were or what they did behind closed doors; their ability to keep their kids off the street protected them.

Later in the trial I was asked what the parents should have done differently, which I thought was an unfair question. Given the circumstances, I said, I believe that Jonathan's parents had done their best, but if Jonathan had been my child, I would have done whatever was necessary to prevent him from going down a wrong path and I would have tried to save his life. This comment prompted Jonathan's mother's abrupt departure from the courtroom; she never spoke to me again. My statement did, however, encourage Jonathan's father, Winston, to testify that he had an affair and that after he became unemployed, he took money from his son when his son was selling drugs. People in this neighborhood tended to have decent values, but the local interaction order intertwined those values with the drug trade, resulting in tacit relationships with that scene. In Winston's case, drug money paid the mortgage so that he could maintain his family. His willingness to admit this fact in court supported his status as a decent man. Jonathan Wilson was found guilty of conspiracy to commit murder of a federal witness, murdering a rival drug dealer, and being an accessory to two other murders, and he was sentenced to life in prison without the possibility of parole. He is currently housed in a federal prison in a northeastern state.

Over time, as I became engaged with Jonathan's family and the neighborhood, I realized that, given his circumstances, this youth was highly susceptible to the drug trade. It became clear to me that Jonathan's story was emblematic of what other young men, along with their relatives and neighbors, had experienced. With Jonathan's case completed, I decided to return to Lyford Street to conduct an ethnographic study. While I was confident after my first visit there that Jonathan's story was typical of the lives of many boys and young men in the neighborhood, I wanted to do more in-depth research in order to comprehend the patterns that were emerging from what men, women, and children told me as they opened their homes to me during the court case. The rest of this book tells that larger story.

TWO

Drug-Dealing Careers

Drug dealing as it occurs on Lyford Street is so well organized that it has taken on the characteristics of a career. As in most occupations, systematic steps are required for young boys to achieve dealer status. In this neighborhood, these steps include doing small favors for dealers and proving trustworthiness; being initiated through early arrest and various loyalty tests; learning to use money systematically (knowing what to charge, barter/exchange, count and give change) and demonstrating this ability to older dealers; learning how to take orders; learning how to keep safe; and learning how to identify customers, which means looking for white visitors to this largely black area. Young boys progress from running errands to working as lookouts for the dealers. They may be asked or told to hold drugs for dealers in emergencies. When they become corner boys and start dealing for themselves, they pass through three more stages.

The youngest and newest dealers work the early morning shift. This is the least lucrative shift and the only one during which the younger children are in school and not available to run errands or act as lookouts. Competence at this position earns boys the right to work the afternoon and then the early evening shifts. Finally, successful dealers move up to the much more lucrative night shift. They are then known as old heads, although most are in their early twenties. Boys are typically arrested several times as they progress, earning kudos for loyalty by refusing to give the police any information. These tests begin early, largely because the sentences for adult drug dealers are so harsh. Many boys find themselves in court between ages eight and sixteen facing juvenile time in order to protect an older dealer, who may be a relative. The dealers I studied are not organized as a gang; they are part of a loose network of relatives and neighbors, but each works independently. According to my informants, several of whom were former dealers, they are independent operators who have autonomy and control and can leave the trade without consequences or pressure from other dealers and suppliers (Adler 1993; Adler and Adler 1983).

Residents of poor urban neighborhoods, like participants in any social space, manage a distinct local interaction order through which they enact identities and behaviors consistent with it—for example, as a neighbor, mail carrier, police officer, social worker, or drug dealer. Although practices related to drug dealing do not become morally normative to people living in this neighborhood, everyone must become skilled in interpreting the verbal and nonverbal cues and managing the identities associated with the space they pass through daily. Dealers, police, stickup kids, social workers, or neighbors—all must become experts in the practices that structure the social order that prevails in this place.

Through reconstructing Jonathan's story, I became particularly interested in learning how neighborhood factors shape the daily lives, identities, and interactions of young drug dealers. Collecting ethnographic data about drug-dealing careers required me to observe the social practices on the street and to interview family members and other residents in order to understand the forces shaping boys' and young men's options and decisions. While walking around the neighborhood, I would hand out my business card and ask residents whether they were willing to talk about their community. Although much of my information came from a dozen or so key informants, observation of the neighborhood and the chance social contacts that afforded also produced a great deal of information. My work with local social service agencies facilitated participant observation and allowed people to get to know me in return. After volunteering at a summer day camp run by a local church, I was referred to a community outreach organization close to Lyford Street that provided services to neighborhood residents. After explaining my research project, I volunteered there for two years, organizing community meetings and fund-raisers. The staff included a police officer, a social worker, and a volunteer secretary.

Two key informants in addition to Jonathan were, or had been, involved in drug careers. Fred was a fifty-two-year-old drug user who worked part-time as a laborer and lived two blocks from Lyford Street. He introduced me around the neighborhood as "the professor" and connected me with Dave, his main cocaine dealer. I initially met Fred when I was looking for long-term residents familiar with the drug scene. Fred recognized me and knew about my earlier visits while I was working on Jonathan's defense team. It also helped that I bore some resemblance to Fred's eldest son, who was born when Fred was nineteen. I began by taking Fred out to lunch and asking him about his life and the changes in the neighborhood. It was three months before Fred would divulge anything about his history of drug use or his long-term dealer, Dave. I think Fred introduced me to Dave in order to help me with my study. The connection was made when Fred picked up a small amount of cocaine from Dave, and again later when he took me to a gym where they worked out together. Dave, who had started out on the corner, worked as an independent dealer. He told me that he had built a loyal clientele of cocaine users, but after the legalization of marijuana elsewhere in the United States he also provided high-quality marijuana and ecstasy for his long-term clients. This side business eventually allowed him to leave Lyford Street. Dave's clients were all, by his description, hardworking people.

Before I met Dave, Fred told him that I was writing a book about Lyford Street. Dave, who is three years younger than I am, was initially hesitant to talk to me about anything related to the neighborhood. Yet he found me interesting, largely because I had a Ph.D. A graduate of Bristol Hill High School, Dave was well read, particularly in black history and Islam, and was interested in various theories of how the world worked. He turned out to be as curious about the academic world as I was about the world of drug dealers in Bristol Hill. I was someone he could bounce his ideas off. Initially, in his eyes, I was also a potential cocaine customer. When he attempted to sell me cocaine, I said no. But given my desire to gain Dave's trust and not to insult his occupation, I explained my close family members' drug history; my brother and my nephew were both in prison at that time, and I had no desire for any experiences with cocaine. Dave eventually became a key source of information. Over the next few months, Dave read drafts of my papers, commenting on what I got right and what I got wrong concerning the drug trade on Lyford Street.

Dealing on the Street

The neighborhood is one place by day and another at night. On weekdays at 5:00 p.m., everything seems to change. There is more traffic, the noise level rises, and more people are out walking. Outsiders and patrol officers leave; so do missionaries and social workers. Residents who work outside the neighborhood during the day return home. After one set of outsiders is gone, another set appears: a steady stream of customers drives into the neighborhood between the end of the normal workday and midnight. To get a sense of the flow of daily life, I observed Lyford Street at different times of the day and from different places. I watched the dealers' regular shift changes and saw them being resupplied with drugs. I also observed residents leaving and returning home to see how they managed proximity to dealers, monitored the influx and exit of visitors, and noticed how time changed the social order of places and situations.

Lyford Street is located just off a major expressway, with an entrance to the highway at one end of the street and an exit from the highway at the other, giving buyers from the wealthy suburbs surrounding Bristol Hill easy access and egress. The drug corners in the neighborhood are located in such a way that purchasers can get off the expressway, buy their drugs while remaining in their cars, and then return to the expressway quickly.

The location would not matter so much if the customers lived in or near the neighborhood, but they are almost all from out of town and almost all white. These buyers are rarely caught. Law enforcement efforts concentrate on the dealers, even though without customers there would be no dealers. A police officer who patrols Lyford Street told me that earlier efforts to focus on the buyers were halted following complaints that they involved racial profiling of white visitors to this black neighborhood. Dealers could be seen flagging down any cars that drove by slowly or had white occupants. The lighting on these streets comes mostly from houses and car headlights because the dealers shoot out the streetlights or hire "maintenance" men to dismantle them. Nonetheless, white customers are very noticeable. The double stops required are a familiar feature of the routine. The first stop is to place an order and pay; the second stop is to pick up the drugs.

The strategy of having a team of three working each deal, only one of whom touches the drugs, and then only for a few seconds, makes it very difficult for the police to make significant arrests. While drug dealing is illegal, it is nonetheless closely tied to the overall economy. For instance, competition between dealers increased during the economic downturn in the fall of 2008, and I witnessed dealers chasing after cars trying to get their business. The shared understanding that the dealers all live on Lyford Street meant that dealers who worked the block tolerated competition only from neighboring dealers. Nevertheless, competition among them could become quite fierce.

Identifying Features of Drug-Dealing Areas

Several visible features identify this neighborhood as a place for drug dealing: graffiti, vacant lots, gym shoes hanging suspended from electrical wires at corners, broken streetlamps, and strategically placed small piles of trash.

Graffiti expresses broadly shared community sentiment. The most elaborate are murals memorializing drug dealers, innocent bystanders, and valued members of the community who died as a consequence of the drug trade. They symbolize both community solidarity and the sacrifices that some members of the community are seen as making for others in a high-risk game. Vacant lots are often created through the concerted efforts of upstanding citizens who hoped to curb the spread of drug dealing by having the city tear down vacant houses. Thus, vacant lots are evidence of residents' collective efficacy, not of neglect. The gym shoes hanging from electrical wires are placed there by dealers to mark the boundaries of drug-dealing areas, and buyers look for them. Even trash plays an important role by providing places to hide drugs and guns; if it is removed, the trash pile will be replenished.

Although the police contend that the community would be better off if the city enforced property codes and removed graffiti, the benefits are debatable. Most houses and yards are kept up fairly well, and neighbors help with cutting grass and cleaning trash when they perceive that someone has a problem maintaining their yard. The worst residential properties are those with high tenant turnover and absentee landlords who do nothing to keep up the property. Fining landlords might work, but fines would be beyond the means of the tenants. Most of the unkempt properties, however, are vacant houses and lots owned by the city and state. The memorial murals, a sacred type of graffiti, are a special case. Removing them would be offensive. They are a valued representation of community sentiment toward a deceased person whom residents perceive as wrongfully killed and who is still mourned by those who live nearby.

Indeed, these murals and memorials on Lyford are one of the more noticeable results of solidarity and collective action in this community. These memorials, which are created at the site where death occurred, are of two types. The first are murals for drug dealers. These tend to be large, elaborate, and relatively permanent; the oldest on Lyford Street commemorates a death in 2003. Not every drug dealer who is killed earns a mural. They indicate a measure of respect for the deceased and a recognition that his death was a sacrifice for a drug trade that is created and sustained by locals. During Jonathan's trial, when a prosecutor asked a youth from the neighborhood whether a specific mural honored a particular drug dealer, he answered, "No one would ever paint a mural for that person" and laughed derisively. Jonathan told me forcefully that "assholes don't get murals."

The five murals in the neighborhood span areas up to twelve by eight feet and are painted on the sides of houses, often near drug-dealing locations, as a reminder of both the dangers dealers face and the honored members of the community with whom they share these risks. Like a grave headstone, the murals often give the deceased's dates of birth and death accompanied by

"RIP." Other messages include "in memory of," "we love you," "real niggas hold you down," and "we miss you." The murals are colorful and well done. The artists often signed and dated them on Lyford Street. These murals illustrate a sense of solidarity as well. The "real niggas" are those who truly know you; in doing so, they support you as well. These memorials carry significant meaning for community members, and when outsiders treat them as anything less than sacred objects they are actively denying that deep meaning and the role they play in community life—ironically, further increasing the solidarity of insiders.

The memorials for "innocent" bystanders are very different from those for drug dealers. Temporary collections of cards, teddy bears, and candles around telephone poles and lampposts memorialize bystanders and other valued members of the community who were killed by the violence associated with drug dealing. As with the drug dealers, not every victim gets a memorial; they are memorialized if a sufficient number of people view their death as unfortunate, undeserved, or sacrificial. I saw only two bystander memorials during a period when at least four other people were killed by drug-related violence. The vigils held at the memorials are large gatherings that both evoke and symbolize ritual solidarity. Many people attend over a period of several days. That the local drug dealers themselves are not seen as the cause of these deaths is evidenced by their presence at memorial vigils and their positive interactions with other residents there. It is my impression that drug dealers sponsor some of these memorials. People in the neighborhood feel that loss and danger are something everybody is subjected to and nobody has any control over; the fault lies outside the community in the unfair circumstances they are all forced to share, not in the actions of a few community members.

Corner Boys

All of the dealers who sell drugs in Bristol Hill are known as corner boys, although they also work from vacant lots along the street. The corners are the most prominent drug-dealing spots. Dealers need to be easily visible to buyers driving in from the expressway and yet be able to disappear quickly if the police show up (Manning 1977, 1980, 2008). Although dealers are available around the clock, most action occurs between six in the evening and midnight.

On a single shift, two or three dealers work a spot together. The first is an order taker and money collector. He identifies the buyer, takes a drug order and cash, and communicates the order and pickup location to a second member of the team. That person retrieves the drugs, which are usually stashed in small amounts throughout the block under bits of trash or rocks. He takes out only the amount of drugs required for that purchase and delivers it directly to the customer. The order taker and drug deliverer are usually in close-enough proximity to see each other, and typically the order taker sends the customer's car toward the drug deliverer. If surveillance becomes a problem, then the process becomes more complicated. For instance, the buyer could be directed to a more obscure pickup spot or be told to show up somewhere else at a specified time. The third person, a lookout, circles constantly, watching for police and customers. It is more difficult to identify this third person, but informants told me that they are almost always there on Lyford Street. Certain children and teenagers walk around the neighborhood for the dealers, keeping an eye out for customers and law enforcement.

Although dealers usually dress extremely well and in the latest fashion when they are not dealing drugs, they wear something like a uniform while they are working. In the summer they dress alike in white T-shirts and tank tops and dark pants or shorts. In the winter they wear black Dickies or carpenter pants and black hooded sweatshirts. While these outfits mark them as drug dealers, they also make it very difficult for the police to distinguish dealers from one another; from a distance, they all look alike. In a chase, for instance, the police might start out after one dealer and end up catching someone else. Dealers choose locations with many escape routes and poor lighting so they have an advantage. Since only one of the three team members is ever holding drugs, they can switch places and prevent the police from catching them with anything (Manning 1980).

I was sometimes able to observe top dealers who supplied all the corner boys. They usually remained mobile, circling the block during the day and resupplying drugs when dealers ran low. They did not carry the drugs with them but directed dealers to locations where drugs were hidden. Most of the drugs were stored in vacant houses, under cars, and in bags that resembled trash. Not having drugs in their houses or cars or on their persons protected them from stickups as well as arrests.

Since the quantities at each location were small, if a dealer was caught, the loss would be limited; so too, at least theoretically, would be the punishment. Guns were considered an important tool, but the penalty for being caught with a gun made it too dangerous to carry one while working. Dealers handled the guns the same way they did the drugs. Most shared guns that were hidden close by but never kept them on their person. The practice of storing drugs and guns in public places where the kids in the neighborhood could see them bound the kids to the dealers' code. Protecting these public spaces from predatory outsiders was essential.

The Youngest Dealers on the Day Shift

Although the morning hours between eight and ten were the slowest in terms of drug dealing, I enjoyed watching kids go off to school and adults leave for work and witnessing the arrival of other people who worked in the neighborhood, such as trash collectors, city maintenance staff, electricians, and social workers. This was my favorite time of day because the morning drug dealers tended to be the youngest and the least threatening. They didn't bother me, and I didn't bother them. According to Dave, morning is the worst time to be out selling drugs; there are fewer drug buyers, no cover, and no younger helpers. This shift is left to the youngest dealers.

When dealers took breaks, the corner was unoccupied for ten or fifteen minutes, and I could take field notes and photograph the spots where they worked. I tried to walk around the neighborhood in such a way that I could make observations without being noticed by the dealers. I was especially careful not to do anything that would draw the attention of the more powerful dealers and suppliers. Most of my photographs were taken during the day, when drug sales were infrequent. On some streets I slowed my pace; on others I hurried. In accord with the code of the street, I never made direct eye contact with dealers, even when they were being helpful, and on the few occasions when we did cross paths I spoke only if spoken to. Whether out of ritual or curiosity, the older dealers would sometimes greet me and I would then return their greetings.

The dealers working the afternoon shift are a little older and more trusted by the suppliers and adult dealers. School-age children are around in large numbers to run errands and serve as lookouts. The pace of selling drugs picks up, but because it is still daylight, the dealers work in full view. The risk of arrest is higher than at other times. Older dealers who work this shift might do so in the role of order taker, without coming into contact with drugs at any time. The children play an important protective role here, and they are available to hold drugs for older dealers being chased by the police.

Old Heads on the Night Shift

The old heads, those who have proven themselves as dealers, are no longer juveniles; if caught, they serve time. They are also more likely to have prior records and draw longer sentences if arrested and convicted. Working after dark gives them some cover from the police. Since they are making more money, they are much more likely to become the targets of stickups. The risks increase enormously for dealers as they progress up the career ladder.

At the same time, more experienced dealers take more precautions. I was unable to make extended observations at night because it was too dangerous. From the observations I did make, I could see the same teamwork that characterized the daytime shifts. But most of my information about the older dealers comes from informants.

Groups of old heads were known to seize drugs and money from other dealers by brute force. At times, I was told, they would accost their chosen victim and torture him until he revealed where his major stash was located. Since the location of the stash was secret and yet in a public place away from their own location, it was never guarded.

The proliferation of guns on the street is due in part to the extreme danger of dealing. Guns are used to protect a dealer's drug supply from stickups and addicts—not necessarily their own clients. Dealers also rely on guns in an effort to keep their families safe. They may use guns to collect payments from customers buying on credit or to punish an addict or rival dealer who steals drugs from a stash spot. Pistol-whipping addicts and customers for stealing or for failing to pay is a common practice. A drug dealer who does not protect his "face"—that is, his honor and reputation on the street—will not last long. Buying and exchanging guns is relatively easy for anyone. Because the guns are not kept on dealers' persons, anyone wanting to use one must first test it to see if it is loaded and will fire. Firing guns in the air to make sure they work and to elicit fear accounts for most of the frequent gunshots heard in this neighborhood.

Vacant Lots and Playgrounds

In the neighborhood around Lyford Street, public space and open space are treated quite differently. Despite a widespread belief that drug dealing occurred in public parks, making them unsafe, I never observed drug dealing in any public space. Several informants confirmed this fact. Indeed, public spaces were poor locations for drug dealing. Drug dealing occurs in open spaces with easy access and egress, while public space is usually fenced in and centrally located. Residents seem to avoid official public spaces, while nevertheless doing their business in public. Spaces designated for public use in this neighborhood are, in any case, extremely limited. The last remaining playground in the neighborhood was demolished in 2008.

I heard two different accounts from officials about why the playground was demolished. Their explanations suggest not only the stereotypes that outsiders impose on Lyford Street but also how the bureaucracy rationalizes its own unjustifiable actions. Initially, the police alleged that the playground was dangerous for children and an eyesore. A city employee who did not live in the community claimed that the park was unfit for children to play in. He put it on a demolition list, and less than a week later it was gone. When asked why he had the park torn down, he said it was not because of the play structure, which was safe, but because of the "negative element" that he claimed hung out there. When pressed, he asserted that the park had become a "haven for drugs, murderers, and dead bodies." No violence had ever occurred in the playground, however. Ironically, most of the murders and drug deals that occurred in this neighborhood took place near vacant lots like the one that had just been created. After the playground's demolition, the city produced a report stating that it was condemned for safety reasons such as bad lighting.

The park was hardly a suitable spot for drug dealing. It was surrounded on three sides by a high fence, behind which stood houses with their backs to the playground. The fourth side faced a street that was separated from the highway by a service road. There was only one gate through the fencing. To reach the playground, a car coming from the highway would have had to drive deep into a dark and uninhabited part of the neighborhood, which would not appeal to white suburbanites. Unfortunately, the park was equally badly situated for use by children. Parents were reluctant to allow their children to play there, even though the playground was well equipped, because they could not see them from their front windows or access it through their yards. The playground was always deserted, although once I saw a few adults sitting and talking there in the dark. Three weeks after the demolition of the park, the city received a grant to build a new playground, but it was not located in this neighborhood.

The rationale of deterring crime was also used as a justification for removing the bus shelters from this neighborhood, which was done just before the playground was demolished. Observing this process provided some insight into how other public spaces in Bristol Hill had been dismantled over time. The irony is that this systematic effort to eliminate public spaces to prevent interaction with drug dealers forced people to interact on the street—where the dealers are active. The practice of dismantling and demolishing public spaces has created many vacant lots, which are overgrown with grass and deliberately strewn with trash. Residents, very few of whom own cars, must routinely walk by vacant lots where guns and drugs are hidden.

How Interaction Orders Shape Individuals' Choices

While participants in orderly social settings can exercise some choice over the actions they perform, the social situation and the expectations it generates frame their choices. What they do and do not do is interpreted by others in predetermined ways, regardless of their personal motivations or intentions. Equally important, social settings are organized around commonly understood practices that constrain the alternatives open to participants. The interaction order leaves most people with very little choice over the set of practices they engage in. Although those who occupy privileged positions often operate under the delusion that they have the power to decide their own course, few black people who live in poverty can maintain this illusion.

The code of the street is buttressed by a set of background expectations (Garfinkel 1967) through which residents organize social interaction in their neighborhood. Unless we comprehend the compulsions of this local interaction order, we cannot understand what happens to children who grow up there. Analyzing actions that take place in neighborhoods like Lyford Street without context and according to external standards is a fundamental error. Everyone who lives in the neighborhood must become oriented to the situated practices through which the code of the street is implemented, whether they like it or not. Under such conditions, the idea that a child chooses to become involved in criminal activities is wide of the mark. Unless the entire matter of drug-dealing careers is approached differently, the desperate conditions that exist in places like Lyford Street will continue to produce an endless supply of young black men to fill our prisons.

The local order on Lyford Street both constructs and enables the choices and resources that are available to people. The specific location in which people find themselves can profoundly shape their personal feelings and attitudes. Focusing on how the locally situated character of the social order that composes daily life frames the choices and resources available to people is an important corrective to the preconception that individuals choose their situations or that their attitudes and values shape those situations. This tight framing of the possibilities for daily interaction leads to another characteristic of Lyford Street and neighborhoods like it: a profound contradiction between the beliefs residents hold and the practices they engage in. Because practices rather than beliefs drive the orderliness of social action, there is always some discrepancy between the norms and actions (Anderson 2002; Rawls 2000, 2009). On Lyford Street, this contradiction took an extreme form. Because the practices that so closely circumscribe daily interaction support an illegal activity that conflicts with residents' deeply held values, they have no opportunity to act on their values. This fundamental contradiction between beliefs and behavior does not reflect on the moral character of individuals.

The social order of such neighborhoods rests on the nature of the underground or illegal economic enterprise and the orderly practices necessary to succeed in it, not on what people believe, value, or want for themselves and others. Communities where drug dealing structures the economy have different local order practices than communities where sex work or working off the books are the main illegal enterprises. Understanding how individuals enter these careers requires comprehension of the specific local order that structures the choices available to them (Adler 1983, 1993; Murphy, Waldorf, and Reinarman 1990). Assuming that they have the same choices as middle-class people living in the suburbs is naive. Even assuming that the local order of all neighborhoods where drug dealing flourishes is the same is problematic; the relationship between residents and dealers in small cities like Bristol Hill is significantly different from that in large cities like Chicago.

Money and Guns

In Lyford Street, independent dealers are ranked in a hierarchy based on age and experience. The convergence of multiple actors and the layout of the neighborhood explain why dealers themselves seldom hold drugs or drug money. Several trade practices were apparently designed to limit the potential for lost money and drugs, police raids, arrests, and criminal charges. These include the use of guns, which are stashed near the dealer's corner but, to avoid felony firearms charges, are rarely carried; the constant resupplying of drugs to dealers; the limited amounts of cash carried by dealers; and the division of labor between lookouts and corner boys. According to numerous informants, these ways of controlling losses and arrests developed in response to the legal and informal risks associated with the trade, especially police raids, armed robberies, and sanctions from suppliers who provide drugs on credit. Significantly, the same practices that protect dealers from the police also shield them from being robbed by other criminals, ensuring that, when things go wrong, drug money can easily be repaid and sales are only temporarily disrupted.

Dealers must take into account the risks associated with working in an illegal economy, such as stickups by groups in search of cash and drugs (Contreras 2012). The old heads who supply drugs are highly mobile. Those who are successful are likely to move out of the neighborhood. To avoid being found, they live in properties rented in the names of others, such as parents, girlfriends, relatives, and friends. They can earn about $1,000 to $1,200 a week by selling approximately 2.5 ounces of powder. Some old heads are major suppliers and live in port cities along the East Coast. The corner boys are much more vulnerable to robbery, as well as arrest. These factors limit the amount of money they make.

Gus, a former dealer who had attended Sunday school with Jonathan, described the cash exchange and moneymaking practices on Lyford Street. "If my old head was to give me something like a ballgame [3.5 grams of cocaine], you could bag up $200. He would just want $100 off of it or $125, and I would get the rest. Or he might just want $100 and I get $100, so we were both making something off of it." This account is very telling, not only about the large profits to be made on the corner but also about the hierarchy, the potential for credit, and the ability of dealers to negotiate rates of return.

When Jonathan started to become successful at dealing, he became a target for stickups. Stickups are dreaded because when drugs are given on credit, the dealer must pay the supplier even if the drugs or proceeds have been stolen. Most dealers fear stickups as much as they do arrest. The old heads would even target younger dealers as a way of making easy money. To enrich themselves, corner boys have been known to claim that their drugs were stolen while withholding the money from their suppliers. What I witnessed on the corner suggests that this tactic is rarely successful: drugs supplied on credit must be paid for, regardless of raids or robberies.

Jonathan was held up after a man he had known most of his life, a prominent old head who worked as a bus driver at night and sold cocaine on the side, took him to a house in an expensive neighborhood that he pretended was his. Standing at the door of the house without going in, the man appeared to take Jonathan under his wing, explaining the rules of the drug game and how to turn a major profit, assuring Jonathan that he too could have such a house. While the old head was winning Jonathan's trust, Jonathan volunteered information such as how much "weight" he was moving, where he kept his stash, and how much money he made in a month. Jonathan later discovered that the man had set him up to be robbed. When he was tipped off by an older dealer, he remembered the encounter and the information he willingly volunteered. After the robbery, Jonathan became more covert and less trusting of those around him.

Drug Careers Rarely End Well

The experiences of youths like Jonathan reveal an interaction order of drug dealing on Lyford Street that sweeps up most boys and young men who live there. The sense they learn to make of daily life in this space, which is necessary to navigate the street safely, inexorably draws them into drug dealing.

The rule of law is not only at odds with the code of the street but frequently, although unpredictably, disrupts the order that normally exists there. Dealers must routinely manage a terrain filled with complex situations that blur the line with regard to the rule of law, the work requirements of drug dealing, and the expectations of those who live in the neighborhood. Unfortunately, the criminal justice system does not recognize the social order that exists in places like Lyford Street as a force that shapes young men's options or take it into account as a mitigating factor when they are charged with drug offenses. These ordered practices are by definition illegal, and once brought under the gaze of law enforcement agencies, they are sanctioned as though the participants had the same choices available to middle-class youths.

The situated contexts and interactional moves involved in selling drugs on Lyford Street compose the order of this neighborhood. The social identities that are possible to construct in this community are severely constrained by the lack of job opportunities produced by long-term economic decline and compounded by arrest records that are nearly universal. The violence that erupts periodically entails incalculable risks, but does not weigh as heavily on young men as their chronic economic exclusion. Managing and performing social identity is always a situation-specific process, however, and knowing what the available identities are does not explain how and why people adopt them.

Most seriously, the social order that exists on Lyford Street cannot be counted on. A level of unpredictability remains, creating a situation in which nothing can ever be taken for granted. As Harold Garfinkel (1967) argued, being able to take social orders for granted is one of the foundations of understanding, trust, and stability in social life. When nothing can be assumed, social life has a fragile edge that makes it very different from more conventional social arrangements.

The street's social activity is highly predictable between incidents, but drug-related crime and the incursions of law enforcement make it impossible to know how things will transpire from one moment to the next, much less over the long term. Consequently, people in the neighborhood maintain a constant vigilance and laser-like focus on the present. The need to gauge the uncertainties surrounding a drug deal gone sour, a robbery, or even a murder, all of which carry the equally unpredictable risk of police involvement and arrest, constitutes the local interaction order. Over time, tactics geared toward immediate survival become paramount, limiting planning for the future and precluding extended consideration of the potential consequences of present behavior.

Fundamentally, in consonance with the exigencies of the local inter-action order, the near-total lack of access to mainstream economic and so-cietal resources in neighborhoods like this places most people in situations with little autonomy and control over their everyday lives. Having a job and living one street away from a drug-dealing corner does not insulate anyone sufficiently or exempt them from the necessity of understanding and nego-tiating the interaction order. Employment or homeownership may make certain aspects of living more predictable, but the infrastructure supporting much of daily life in the neighborhood remains uncertain. People must enter and exit the neighborhood. Their children must go to school and play with other children. Their homes are within reach of bullets from drug deal-ers' guns. Proximity to the underground economy of drug dealing and the social systems that support it makes it very difficult for anyone to escape.

The embedded local order of the drug scene shaped Jonathan's entry into drug dealing. His life history offers a vantage point from which to under-stand the community as a whole. The organization of the neighborhood, its position in the economy, the location of access and escape routes, and the intricate familial and friendship networks produce a social environment that facilitates the recruitment and training of dealers. Induction into drug dealing involves learning many valuable skills that would contribute to these men's success in legal occupations if any were available. A successful career in the drug trade requires mastering multiple tasks and calculating risks and benefits in an environment that, despite its ordinary orderliness, remains unpredictable (Laub and Allen 2000).

Comprehending these local social forces offers a valuable perspective on Jonathan's involvement in the drug trade and its effects on his life and that of his family. Jonathan is not merely a victim of circumstances, but many of his actions and choices are intelligent and rational given his circumstances. Community members' lenient attitude toward drug dealing is influenced by their understanding of young men's marginal position relative to the main-stream economy. In other words, although boys' involvement may stem from familiarity with and proximity to the local order of drug dealing, their continued commitment to it as adults, despite their experiences of arrest and imprisonment, is reinforced by their inability to secure other means of earn-ing a livelihood. Neighborhood narratives of drug-dealing careers seldom mention incarceration and an untimely death. In the face of these risks, and even the many factors that limit their incomes, they still see drug dealing as the best—or even the only—option available to them.

The interaction-order practices associated with drug dealing offer a deep and shared sense of collective identity and local solidarity. The more embattled people are, the deeper their commitment may become. Neighbor-hood residents see the same scenarios unfolding, whether they like them or not. By contrast, the motivations of outsiders may be hard to understand. When people feel that outsiders rarely have their best interests in view, the fact that the local order comes from inside and belongs to them may give it a positive value even when it supports activities they do not believe in. In this way, inequality produces enclaves of people who embrace forms of order that protect them from the mainstream—but in so doing maintain or even increase their marginality, thus running counter to broadly democratic principles. By creating the necessity of retreating into protective enclaves, socioeconomic inequality can destroy democracy and generate physical and mental barriers between classes and racial-ethnic groups. Outsiders neither interact with people in these communities nor perceive the conditions that exist there, while at the same time creating policies that simultaneously pro-duce and punish them.

THREE

The Rise and Fall of Lyford Street

In 1994 many poor black families moved to Lyford Street after the temporary closure of all of the city's public housing. The neighborhood was already in decline and had an embedded drug scene, but in retrospect the sudden influx of this new group of poor people appeared to be responsible for its deterioration—at least in the minds of longtime residents. While their advent may have speeded up the departure of white and black middle- and working-class families, they were not the primary culprits in the neighborhood's decline. Although the projects had hosted a drug trade, Lyford Street dealers were in place long before the arrival of their less well-off counterparts. The exodus of white residents, the arrival of a large cohort of poor families, and the continued contraction in the job market coincided. Focusing on what was most immediately visible rather than on the underlying causes in the economy and public policy, the dominant narrative identified the newcomers as the source of the decline. While the ways residents make sense of local history are extremely important, blaming those who came from public housing lets the responsible parties off the hook. The local narrative that attributes the neighborhood's demise to people from the projects not only provides a recognizable story for residents but also creates solidarity by making common sense of shared experiences.

While this consensus view contains many clues about the history of the neighborhood, it is inconsistent with the recorded facts. Some discrepancies are obvious. For example, Jonathan Wilson's father blamed his son's involvement in the drug trade on people from the projects, but Jonathan began dealing at least six years before their arrival. The neighborhood around Lyford Street mirrored Bristol Hill's loss of population, a consequence of protracted economic decay. Many residents had departed prior to the closing of the projects, allowing the city to move displaced tenants into empty units.

Longtime residents remember the mass influx but not the previous exodus, which was decades in the making. Lyford Street's decline does not represent an instance of the shuffling of the poor. Nonetheless, the story that circulates in the neighborhood matters, for it blames the drug problem on others who came from elsewhere rather than on the local community.

The discrepancies between the accounts presented to me and the history revealed in the records prompted me to analyze the process of neighborhood change more carefully. How did Lyford Street shift from a predominantly white middle-class neighborhood to a poor black community? What relationship, if any, was there between the changing racial composition of the neighborhood and the drug scene that became deeply embedded in it? Why are narratives that blame the poor for the neighborhood's decline so common? I explored the shifts in its racial and class composition between 1943 and 2010 by using archival data and residents' narratives, which voice differing perceptions of the causes of these dramatic changes.

To unlock the mystery of the drug trade, neighborhood decline, and demographic shifts in the neighborhood, I spoke with people who witnessed these processes from beginning to end. I was able to locate original residents of Lyford Street, both black and white, by studying historical migration patterns and through word of mouth. The accounts of the first white families to move to Lyford Street—all of whom have since relocated, many to surrounding suburban areas—are helpful in understanding these changes. So are those from the first set of black families to move in, two of whom still live there today. I take an in-depth look at the ways in which residents of both races tend to describe the causes of neighborhood decline, from the rise in criminal activity, vacant dwellings, and substandard housing conditions to the personal failings of tenants receiving rent subsidies under the Section 8 housing voucher program.

The Neighborhood

Proposed in 1940, Lyford Street was a suburban-style housing development on the outskirts of Bristol Hill. Lyford Street predates similar communities such as Levittown, built in Pennsylvania in 1952. Although located in Bristol Hill proper, Lyford Street is situated two miles from downtown, and its housing design is similar to many suburban communities being planned at that time. Most residents used FHA loans to buy their own homes, which sold for an average of $4,400 in 1943; with only a 10 percent down payment and low fixed-interest rates, these thirty-year mortgages were affordable even for working people. Two years later, government funds were used to build a supposedly temporary public housing project adjacent to the neighborhood. These public housing units, which were originally inhabited by members of white ethnic groups who had lived in slums along the river, were not replaced as quickly as had been planned. The construction of a major highway separated the projects from the neighborhood around Lyford Street. Margaret Upton, a seventy-one-year-old former resident who is white, recounted:

> It was the middle of the war, World War II, and they were told there was no available housing in the major city because of the war, so they secured housing in what's called Bristol Hill on Lyford Street. I was born in Bristol Hill Hospital, and so my first eighteen months were spent in Bristol Hill. My parents had neighbors who were receiving the *New York Times*, which told them that these [neighbors] would be friends. So they made friends with this family named the Tapperts. The father eventually became an executive in an airline company. They were almost like us, you know—higher level than my parents—but they maintained a friendship for years, like forty years after that.

Madeline Hopper, an original resident of English and German descent who was eighty-seven when I interviewed her, stated that Lyford Street was not only overwhelmingly white but also devoid of white ethnics, a distinction she made when I asked her about local racial demographics. Madeline declared that even the Poles, Italians, and Ukrainians, some of whom moved into the nearby public housing projects, were seen as nonwhite. When I asked her whether it was a predominantly white community when she moved there, she replied:

> That's what I asked my friend Suzanne. She said, "I never gave it a thought." She said, "They were just people we lived with. They were our neighbors and friends." [*Laughs.*] I said, "I can't believe you would ask a question like that, because back in the forties and fifties when we lived there, it was different. Your Italians were across town because they had their own churches. . . . They had their own schools, their own stores. They ate food differently than what the Polish ate, the Polish and Ukrainians. They had the same thing: their own schools, their own churches, their own little stores. World War II, they [white ethnics] started to integrate."

According to Madeline, these white ethnics became incorporated into the community after World War II and the Korean War.

To understand the development of this community, we must consider the racial and class segregation in housing that existed during the 1930s in this region, as it did throughout the United States (Massey and Denton 1993). Following the Great Depression, municipal governments and social service agencies were encouraged to assist in the elimination of slums and the provision of decent housing. Government officials in Bristol Hill, recognizing the inadequate living conditions of more than five hundred poor black families and two hundred immigrant families in the area, commissioned a report that characterized their riverside neighborhoods as slums deserving of demolition. The overcrowded wood-framed "shacks" lacked indoor plumbing and electricity, making them a public health hazard. In addition, a survey conducted by two Protestant human-service agencies highlighted the need for public utilities and for educational, health care, and recreational facilities.

Equally important, blacks and whites lived side by side. The fact that this riverside neighborhood was racially integrated aroused no special comment, but the public housing that replaced it in the 1940s was racially segregated by design. In describing the slums, eighty-two-year-old Janice Watkins, who is black and whose family moved to Bristol Hill in the 1920s, stated: "It was nothing for us to have white people at our dinner table. My father, he had a great big Bible, and he would sit there and read the Bible with them and my mother would feed them." The city built four public housing developments, three for blacks and one for immigrants and ethnics of European descent, containing a total of approximately 1,250 public housing units in the 1940s.

Bristol Hill was heavily hit by the post–World War II decline in the area (Woldoff 2011; Sugrue 2014; Pattillo 2007). Simultaneously, white residents relocated to suburban areas that were predominantly or exclusively white. The private housing market, like public housing policy, promoted racial segregation (Massey and Denton 1993; Sugrue 2014). While I found no evidence of restrictive covenants, the clear racial boundaries that exist in Bristol Hill today are a legacy of state-sponsored segregation and the private practices of whites who separated themselves not only from black people but also from the poor. For those who left the slums, moving to all-white public housing was a step up the social scale; for those who moved to suburbs like Bristol Hill, the incomes of their neighbors reflected positively on their own status.

In Bristol Hill, many black people who had resided in the projects pointed to the class diversity that had initially existed there. Over time, they explained, the projects became places of concentrated poverty as the eligibility requirements for public housing changed. When I asked about the projects, residents named prominent politicians, judges, lawyers, and physicians who grew up there. Many areas of the city that were racially segregated began to integrate as housing legislation passed. The Fair Housing Act of

1968 (Title VIII of the Civil Rights Act) prohibited discrimination on the basis of race, color, sex, national origin, religion, family status, or disability in renting and buying homes. Fair housing created an opportunity for the first black families to move into the all-white public housing development adjacent to Lyford Street, as well as the Lyford Street neighborhood itself. After the integration of private housing, public housing integration soon followed. At first, many white residents were resistant to black families moving into the all-white projects. In contrast, Madeline Hopper and other black newcomers pointed out that when they moved to Lyford Street, their white neighbors were very welcoming.

The first black families arrived in the neighborhood after the passage of housing antidiscrimination laws in 1968. Historical statistics reveal the timing of the demographic shift: in 1970 Lyford Street was 95 percent white; by 1980 the neighborhood was 65.4 percent white and 33.5 percent black. This trend continued, and in 2010 the neighborhood was 12 percent white and 77.1 percent black. This process took place throughout Bristol Hill, along with a dramatic drop in population from 68,000 in 1950 to 33,000 today (U.S. Census 2010). Like many older cities in the northeast, Bristol Hill has lost its affluent residents, although the surrounding suburbs are among the wealthiest in the country.

By 1980 the once all-white public housing units had become all black. Many of the white residents of the projects relocated to a small community that borders Bristol Hill and shares the same school district. Today it remains a largely poor and working-class white neighborhood, and most houses are owner occupied. It is ironic that poor whites who lived with blacks in the slums prior to the building of the housing projects moved out of public housing in large numbers when the Fair Housing Act created an opportunity for the projects to be integrated. While they fled to all-white areas, their black former neighbors moved to Lyford Street. Racial separation, then, has resulted even from policies intended to promote integration.

Lyford Street, along with Bristol Hill proper, experienced a long period of deterioration after the mid-1960s as manufacturing jobs departed. Unemployment became a chronic condition. The official unemployment rate, which does not include discouraged workers who have given up on looking for a job, has never fallen below 20 percent since 1980. The high unemployment rate cannot be explained by deindustrialization alone, however. New industries in the form of prisons, paper mills, hospitals, trash incinerators, weapons manufacturers, and casinos have taken the place of the shipyards and automobile factories. But the competition for these jobs comes from the whole region, not just Bristol Hill. To put it simply, there are not enough jobs to support all of the people in the region. The problems that plague Lyford Street originated in a history of racial discrimination in both employment and housing.

These problems continue to be compounded by public policies that are ill conceived and undemocratic. When I volunteered with a city agency in 2009, a neighborhood beautification project was implemented with a budget of $50,000. The city wanted to install new address numbers on the houses, install and replace lamps on front walks, and conduct minor repairs. The program's implementation was met with resistance, as tenants who were renting from private owners, rather than the city and state, complained that their landlords were not performing basic repairs on dysfunctional plumbing, leaky roofs, and broken windows or providing pest control. The funds allocated for repairs were supposed to be spread over all 746 homes, but the money ended up going to only 10 residents, all of whom were homeowners who attended community meetings. The question of the relative effectiveness of private action versus public policy is hotly debated, but the interconnection of these two factors is important to examine. Municipal and federal politics related to public housing policy, combined with whites' commitment to racial exclusivity, are responsible for introducing and maintaining racial segregation. Equally important, these policies were implemented in a way that failed to take into account their effects on local cultures. Residents' narratives rest on a strong belief that the causes of segregation are more related to racial differences and class positioning than to public policy. Although these sentiments are often misplaced, their accounts are vital in understanding how the community makes sense of neighborhood changes.

The Dominant Local Narrative about Lyford Street's Decline

Mr. John was among the very first black people who moved to the Lyford Street neighborhood in the late 1960s. He described the process of the neighborhood decline this way: "The neighborhood started turning. And I'll tell you exactly when it started turning. It started turning when they started closing down the projects. Until they started closing down the projects, you'd have one [black] family here, one [black] family there, which was cool by me. But when they started closing down the projects, instead of that one family moving in, you had five, six families moving in. And white people started getting up and fleeing. I'm not going to say moving; they were fleeing. And I used to sit back and I used to say, 'Well, you know, I'm black. They didn't flee when I moved in.'"

In many ways Mr. John's recollection is correct: the exodus of whites from Lyford Street was a long, drawn-out process that was not noticeable until the arrival of large numbers of black families who had been relocated from public housing. But on Lyford Street, as in the city of Bristol Hill as a whole, demographic changes were part of a larger trend of population decline. Although the causal connections between these developments are complex and multidimensional, the stories that residents tell enable us to better understand how community members make sense of this place.

A former resident who, like Mr. John, was one of the first blacks to move to Lyford Street recounted that significant demographic change began with the advent of tenants with subsidized housing vouchers. Janice Kelly, who was thirty-eight when I interviewed her and no longer lived in the neighborhood, reported that white residents started leaving and young men clad in "white T-shirts"—that is, drug dealers—began popping up on the corners.

> Not to demonize Section 8 or anything, but Section 8 started coming in, so people who were not homeowners or were not as connected to where they were living. We saw a difference. And I would say . . . we usually tell people, like, the T-shirts. We saw white T-shirts, lots of white T-shirts hanging around the corner. One of the things that kind of disturbed our family was when we found out that when they were destroying some of these places, they were telling the people who were trying to look for, relocate in the city, that they could only use their voucher in the city. It's just something the housing authority was telling people, and that's illegal. They have the right to move wherever they like once they receive a voucher from Section 8. But they were quietly being told, "You're only allowed to move within the city limits."

In this respect, too, federal housing policy was implemented in a way that undermined its stated goals of distributing the poor among middle-class people; steering these low-income families toward Bristol Hill's more impoverished neighborhoods increased the residential concentration of the poor.

While a number of Section 8 tenants moved into the Lyford Street neighborhood, several property owners exploited the vacancies created by the mass exodus by buying properties from homeowners as well as abandoned houses seized by the state because of back taxes or drug activity. A total of five entities outside the state and the city control this fifth of the rental market in the Lyford Street neighborhood. These properties tend to house tenants who are highly transient, and those who own and manage them are notorious for their lack of involvement with those who live there. While residents tended to blame Section 8 tenants as a group, many of their examples of bad neighbors referred to transient tenants who were renting from owners who did not take care of the property.

Josh Kelly, a sixty-year-old former resident of Lyford Street who moved out in the early 1990s, recalled his time in Bristol Hill. "It was not what it is now. I mean, it was poor. There were some white people living in Lyford Street when I was there. That was in the eighties, late eighties, I guess. So, you know, the drug scene, the real scene that you encountered in Lyford Street, was in the projects. Section 8 was just happening. It was still mostly poor homeowners. Renters were just coming in when I was there. So it was a totally different kind of scene. It was relatively safe. I mean, it was Bristol Hill." Josh, who resided in the Lyford Street community prior to the influx of public housing residents, acknowledged that the neighborhood was declining and had a small drug scene before the major influx of public housing tenants. The accounts that blame the drug trade on the people who moved from the projects fail to recognize that both the drug trade and the neighborhood's decline began well before their arrival in the 1990s.

Contemporary Reflections on the State of the Neighborhood

Looking back at the Lyford Street neighborhood in 1980s, one of the first black residents, Irene Walker, now seventy-four, noted its racial diversity and the civility of most of its white residents, even though a number of them began to move from the area. She recounted fond memories of growing up in Bristol Hill, especially the sense of community that existed there and the fact that everything, from homes and cars to food and entertainment, seemed affordable. This sense of economic stability is, regrettably, gone.

Irene Walker also recalled the sense of security she had once experienced in everyday life on Lyford Street; for example, in the past everyone left their doors unlocked. But since the late 1970s, she remarked, the community was no longer quite as "together" as it had once been. She attributed some of these changes to the contemporaneous transformations occurring in the schools. Because many of the teachers at the local schools lived outside the communities in which they taught and did not foster relationships with any of the families in the neighborhood, the school became disconnected from students' parents. Residents who have moved in during the past ten years, particularly mothers of school-age children, also expressed concern about changes in the educational system, including placing fifth- and sixth-graders in the high school. Many worried that young children who had not previously interacted with older children were being exposed to issues that affect more mature youths, including sex and violence. These parents believed that this early matriculation contributed to the high rate of teenage pregnancies. Some residents stated that the local schools made many of these changes without the parents' consent because they knew that the parents would not fight back.

Longtime residents and former residents fondly recalled significant features from the neighborhood's past, including the YMCA, swimming pools, parks, and the skating rink, which have now vanished. In their absence, youths have few constructive or positive ways of spending their spare time; to participate in any of these activities, they must leave town. Some residents recall an increase in violence that coincided with the disappearance of many of these places during the 1960s. Here, too, coincidence is seen as causation; many residents believe that activities that kept children occupied prevented young people from engaging in illegal and dangerous activities. The challenges of raising daughters arouse intense concern, especially given the strong influence of adolescents' peers. Despite parents' attempts to instill their values and instruct their children in wise decision making, adults worried that they could not control the choices their daughters made when they were not under supervision. Some residents discussed contemporary concerns about their sons succumbing to peer pressure to sell drugs. Although these parents raised their sons as best they could, some boys ended up getting into trouble with the police.

Some mothers were sharply critical of the absence of Christian teaching in schools and attributed their children's unruly behavior to this change. For the older generation, their Christian faith is vitally important, not just in the way it has shaped their lives but also in the activities that are offered through the church. Even the secular organizations where I volunteered had to use church facilities, given the lack of space and resources provided by the city. By sharing their gymnasiums and libraries and by offering food pantries and day camps, churches, missionaries, and other religious organizations played substantial roles in providing social services to the poor.

Some longtime residents complained about the rising influence of Muslims not only in Bristol Hill but also the Lyford Street neighborhood. There is a sizable Muslim population in Bristol Hill, and many Muslims utilize services provided by Christian organizations. Some say that the Muslim influence came from prison, as black men who converted while incarcerated brought this faith with them back upon their return. Others say that it originated with an emissary sent by the Nation of Islam to the neighborhood in the 1980s. But the Muslim presence in Bristol Hill is not monolithic. Most Muslims are not affiliated with the Nation of Islam.

Although Lyford Street is predominantly black, some white people reside there, most of whom are missionaries who seek to organize residents to build local churches. One organization, Global Ministries, has been in the neighborhood since the late 1980s, so its activities are well understood. At one time Global Ministries worked exclusively with residents of the projects, focusing particularly on school-age children, but it extended its activities to others when tenants were relocated. The missionaries have long rented a house in vicinity of Lyford Street. They are recognized as local residents, but the association of whiteness with law enforcement, drug addicts, and the church is relevant in everyday interactions. Community members try to reciprocate their good intentions, making sure that nothing bad happens around the homes of ministry workers; although some were broken into in the past, no one was physically harmed.

Stacy, a twenty-four-year-old missionary who lived in the neighborhood, offered this description of Global Ministries:

> We are a Christian mission organization dedicated to planting churches amongst the urban poor. And it's very distinct because it's not just urban folks. Because right now, you know, about new urbanism, young hipsters moving in, taking over neighborhoods, pushing out who's living there, gentrification, and all that stuff, that's not what we're looking at. We're looking at working with those who are on the fringe of an urban area. We go into neighborhoods, and we live there; that's part of what we do—incarnational living, holistic ministry—so we live here. When our roads aren't plowed, our neighbors' roads aren't plowed. We can't drive in from the suburbs where the roads are beautiful in the winter to here, where we're like, "Oh." When it's a problem, it's a problem for us. And that's just the way we see ministry doing best. And it's a lot about redistribution, not only of wealth but resources. So what does that look like when the resources are all just out of touch, out of reach? So, grocery stores, well, there's none in Bristol Hill. So what do we do? We take a van full of moms, when they need it, to the grocery store. Fresh fruits and vegetables? We have a garden, and then we also go to the produce store. We go to the grocery store and get them. But we introduce kids to those things. It's really important. . . . We're going to be starting in the fall a nutrition, a cooking class about nutrition . . . but it's not just going to be me teaching; it's going to be them.

Stacy observed the conjunction of race and poverty and watched the signs of neighborhood change. She had noticed both an increase in the number of Latinos and a nascent process of gentrification, as new people purchased homes and had them renovated. Other white people seemed shocked when she told them where she lived, because it doesn't fit the model of a desirable neighborhood. When I asked what she felt about the attitudes that members of the black community have toward her, she said that because neighborhood residents felt loved unconditionally and received a warm welcome at Global Ministries, they generally showed respect for its members.

Despite the goodwill, the missionaries' whiteness sometimes became an unavoidable attribute in their daily lives. When I asked Stacy whether she had thought about what it means to be white in this neighborhood, she replied:

> I don't necessarily think it's ever been a real issue with those around [us]. Like, it's never like, "Oh, she's the white girl." But internally, I've struggled with it; being white and assumed to be privileged, which I'm not, is something that I struggle with. When I was emceeing the Praise Fest, I really confronted my whiteness, because I'm like, "It's going to be a room full of black people from Bristol Hill. And I'm just some white girl up there. They don't know me. Who am I?" . . . This is people from all different churches. . . . I don't know these people. They don't know me from any other white girl.

Then Stacy recounted an incident she found particularly disturbing.

> I'm driving down Greene Street to go to the store 'cause I wanted to get a soda. . . . You know how the kids stand in the street to collect money for their basketball [or] their drill team? Well, there's this girl standing out there for drill. And I always give them money. Always. If I got it, they get it. I mean, it's so great. Love it. But I didn't have any cash. And I'm actually going to get cash at the store and come back to give it to them. The girl's like, "You white bitch" when I said I didn't have any money. So I pulled the car around. I did a U-turn on Greene Street and Lyford. I got out of the car. I went to their adult leader, and I'm like, "Look, I live up the street. I'm not some white bitch that came down here to get what I need. I'm part of this community, and if your kid's going to talk like that, why would I give your organization money? I was going to get money and bring it back because I think it's important to support this." And she was mortified, and I was very aggressive, because I was already struggling with being white. And when I came back through, they were all on the corner, having a deep conversation [*laughs*] about that issue, you know? You can't say that stuff to people. But it was the first time that somebody had ever really said anything derogatory. When I first moved out here, it was like, "Oh, are you a cop?" "No." "Oh, are you at the church?" "Yep." "Oh, OK."

Like, white people are one of two things: cops or church. But that was the time
I really, really struggled with being white.

This missionary's account is both revealing and insightful. She is aware of
the taken-for-granted notions of whiteness: a position of privilege, a law enforcement officer, a potential drug customer, or a church worker. At the same
time, she is well of aware of the interaction order that is at play in this space
both as a person with a protected identity as a high-status insider-outsider
and as someone who views the children on Lyford Street simply as children.
Her reply to the young girl who called her a white bitch shows not only
that adults can challenge this behavior but that a concerned adult can and
should address it with other adults. From her account of this interaction,
we learn what whiteness does and does not mean in this space. When the
missionary says she is not some white bitch who comes to Lyford Street to
get what she wants, she not only differentiates herself from the whites who
most frequent Lyford Street but recognizes her own obligation to contribute
and stakes her claim for respect as a member of the community. Membership carries privileges that have nothing to do with race. Reciprocity exists
even between the whites and blacks who live on Lyford Street.

On reflection, Stacy suggested that while she is aware that her whiteness
means she begins with outsider status, she has faced more serious internal
struggles because her whiteness makes others erroneously assume that she
comes from a position of privilege. She spoke of being overwhelmed at
times, but utilizing the strong support system offered by her mission organization. She appreciated the sense of community that exists in the neighborhood, despite its dismal reputation. She saw Global Ministries as a vital part
of the support systems that help those who are struggling.

Making Sense of Neighborhood Change

The stories that people tell about their neighborhood enable residents to
make sense of Lyford Street as a place over time. The discrepancies within
their accounts and between their narratives and the publicly available information about the neighborhood's changing composition are also significant. The exodus of white and black middle- and working-class residents
from Lyford Street was over fifty years in the making between 1940 and
1992 and mirrored the population decline and racial shifts in Bristol Hill
as a whole. This gradual, incremental process occurred family by family,
house by house, and attracted little attention among those not directly involved. The dramatic event that people on Lyford Street noticed, by con-

trast, happened all of a sudden: the massive influx of an identifiable group of poorer people to the neighborhood's vacant rental housing in the early 1990s. People who lived on Lyford Street had always kept a certain social distance from those who lived in the projects across the freeway; now they were moving in next door. Residents who witnessed this process had a collective experience of seeing relocation in real time, rather than over time. The newcomers' arrival coincided with the economic decline that was afflicting the entire city. The stories longtime residents tell attribute Lyford Street's drug trade and consequent decline to those who brought this illegal form of making a living with them from the housing projects—without recognizing that similar economic and demographic shifts were already taking place in their own neighborhood and affecting their children.

The social and demographic changes that have taken place in Bristol Hill and the Lyford Street neighborhood involve a complex process of racial-ethnic exclusion, integration, and resegregation with clear warning signs all along the way. The two narratives of Lyford Street and the housing projects tell a story that moves from the integration of white ethnics and middle-class blacks to the failure to integrate the poor. The subsequent flight of poor whites from the projects once they became integrated could have served as a cautionary tale, but the planners who sought to revitalize public housing and disperse poor black families disregarded its lessons, ensuring that what had happened in public housing was replicated as tenants with housing subsidies entered the private market. In this community, resegregation arose from a malign combination of public policy and whites' private practices. Historical records and personal stories can help us to understand the often overlooked, misunderstood, and ever-changing nature of integration, segregation, and racial isolation in urban spaces.

The decline of the Lyford Street neighborhood in the form of white flight, vacant housing, and the drug trade resulted not from the relocation of tenants from the projects but from misconceived and poorly implemented housing policies that segregated blacks and whites and concentrated the poor. Policy makers failed to understand the effects that the displacement of tenants from public housing would have on the Lyford Street neighborhood, the propensity of homeowners to flee changing neighborhoods, and how mass vacancies would impact the housing market. The arrival of more severely impoverished tenants with Section 8 vouchers and the visibility of the drug trade prompted another exodus from the neighborhood.

Understanding how residents make sense of the origins of the present crisis in their neighborhood required an excursion into a history that few people knew, though many were aware of the signal moments when they realized that change was upon them. The interaction-order practices that flourish here have incorporated the newcomers; today few people differentiate between those who came from the projects and those who were there beforehand. The interaction order is also shaped by shared experiences and sense-making, which contribute to the solidarity that exists on Lyford Street. But they all agree that the problems that beset their neighborhood were inflicted upon them by others. While the historical account reconstructed in this chapter is distinct from that offered by residents, it differs mostly in pointing to the political developments that lay behind the visible process of neighborhood change. Policies and practices implemented by outsiders did not improve but rather damaged a densely populated, thriving, and integrated neighborhood, triggering a cascade of negative consequences that continue to this day.

FOUR

Snitching, Gossip, and the Power of Information

How did the longtime and recently arrived African American families in the Lyford Street neighborhood construct and maintain a shared sense of identity? While this process is not visible except in retrospect, the ways in which residents who are and are not involved in the drug trade sustain neighborhood solidarity despite their differing positions reveal the social dynamics of the local interaction order.

Gossip plays a central role in constructing and maintaining community on Lyford Street, as it does in many settings where people interact not only face-to-face but also through others who know them. The gossip network serves as an information-sharing system that makes this neighborhood, with its embedded drug scene, more maneuverable (Rosnow and Fine 1976). Snitching, by contrast, involves insiders going outside the community and giving the police a piece of information. Snitching and gossip are two distinct types of information disclosure, each with its own local politics, that play significant roles in the social organization of the community. Residents who witness an illegal event and tell the police about it are not snitches; snitching requires participation in the illegal activities that are reported. But residents who inform based on gossip alone are distrusted. Gossip tends to occur between insiders and to be positively valued (Rosnow and Fine 1976). Snitching involves outsiders and tends to be penalized. Those who are most concerned with the control of information are those with the most to hide, especially drug dealers and street criminals, whose activities if reported could land them behind bars. Those who have snitched or who might snitch are perceived as very threatening.

When law enforcement agencies encourage residents to break ranks with their community by cooperating with outsiders, it places a great deal of strain on neighborhood solidarity and information sharing by creating distrust, disrupting the flow of information, and evoking stigma and sanctions within the community. By cooperating with law enforcement based on unsubstantiated rumors or mere speculation, informers undermine reciprocity among neighborhood insiders. Cooperation with law enforcement takes many forms. Information can range from an event the person witnessed to a totally fabricated account that falsely but intentionally implicates others. Cooperating with law enforcement based on gossip violates the trust on which social networks rely. Residents are under surveillance from multiple state agencies, including welfare case workers, public housing officials, and probation and parole officers, as well as local police, and violating the rules enforced by these agencies may lead to state penalties. If a person is known to be providing outsiders with information that will lead others to be punished, he or she may be excluded from information-sharing networks. While law enforcement officials are able to achieve a certain level of cooperation in many communities, most officers are unaware of how their presence adversely affects the circulation of information. For the police, information is information; the distinction between gossip and snitching is irrelevant.

Gossip versus Snitching

Cedric, a twenty-nine-year-old former dealer, reported the rules regarding snitching that prevailed on the street, which he learned when he was selling drugs. "'You don't snitch' is the core principle, which everyone knows about. What you do is what you do, and you keep things to yourself; if you get caught, it's your own fault. If you're involved in the game or involved with the person you are providing information about in any way, then you're a snitch. If all parties are involved in criminal activity, then they are all guilty, but if you are not involved, then you have to act in your self-interest."

Dave, who described the politics of snitching very similarly to Cedric, explained the differences between snitching and being a "concerned citizen." "If you are in cahoots with someone on a crime that you get caught for and the other person doesn't and you turn in the other person to get out of trouble, then that's snitching." Yet the contrast ends there, as both men pointed out that calling the police is situational. Dave went on to say that a community member who sees something that isn't right going on but has nothing to do with it is a concerned citizen and not a snitch. Dave thought that men and women handle snitching differently; women often snitch for personal reasons, in a way that is emotional and vindictive, to hurt a person they've had problems with in the past. He saw men's motivation for snitching as more self-interested, although he had noticed some men acting in similar ways as women. I found that local gossip networks are largely gendered, as well as class and cohort based. I did not observe people using these networks vindictively, although Alice Goffman (2014) found that a woman in her study used law enforcement to retaliate against an intimate partner.

Neighborhood gossip is an important and often overlooked form of collective efficacy related to personal safety and neighborhood stability. Longtime residents, particularly homeowners and seniors, use gossip not only for its inherent informational value but also to deal with issues related to neighborhood politics, crime, violence, and personal relationships. Within social networks, gossip passes on both factual information and hearsay and gives residents a chance to clarify misinformation about others and themselves. Gossip networks in this community are organized along lines of gender, class, occupation, and age.

Here, as in many other social settings, information is capital. It can help you prevent your house from being burglarized by people in the neighborhood who prey upon transients. It can be used by various insiders and outsiders to alert authorities when someone is on the run. It can be used to protect a child and punish a parent by reporting an incident of abuse. It can also enable a person to stay out of interpersonal disputes that may end in violence (Katz 2008; Collins 2009).

Two types of accounts circulate locally: detailed narratives told by people who have witnessed a crime, and vague and incomplete stories containing the basic facts that are passed around among third parties. The way information is used in this community has much to do with insider/outsider networks. Insider networks are important, especially because disputes have a tendency to turn violent. Being in an information network that identifies violent actors or warns that a retaliatory act is at play can guarantee a person's safety, while exclusion from it can have serious consequences. Few secrets can exist in a community with long-term kinship and friendship networks that are reinforced by the social isolation that concentrated poverty entails.

The limited access to resources in impoverished communities facilitates the formation of these networks and even encourages mutual aid and reciprocity with regard to information and credible gossip. Being in the know is a matter of life and death. The overall consensus among dealers is that if someone benefits from giving information to the police or informs on an enemy in order to get revenge, they are a snitch. In other contexts, however, information has a recognized order; the ability to keep a secret and not become involved in ongoing disputes is a very valuable form of capital.

Gossip functions in proportion to a source's credibility. Accounts can vindicate, confer shame, generate distrust, and even cast suspicion by circulating unfounded information. Gossip, like snitching, assumes that those who produce accounts are, to some degree, "in the know" as witnesses or participants. Some people effortlessly share information that is ostensibly meant to be kept secret. If someone *wants* a secret to get out, he or she reveals it to these individuals.

A person considered a snitch is generally part of a group that commits a crime and later provides information in hopes of receiving a lighter sentence or exculpating himself entirely. Not all snitches go directly to the police; some discuss private information outside the network with parents, teachers, or friends in a way that will likely lead to intervention, sanctions, and rewards.

Other forms of gossip work more informally and fluidly; they do not carry such stringent sanctions or require having witnessed the event. Unlike snitching, rumors and hearsay can come from nonparticipants. The dealers I interviewed looked down on both snitches who cooperated with law enforcement officials and informers who did not see the crime or participate in it. Here two factors come into play: providing information to those outside the network, and commenting on something that was not witnessed. A resident who witnesses a murder, calls the police, and informs the officers of the offense is not considered a snitch. Those who rely only on hearsay and rumors to produce an account, truthful or not, violate a widely held understanding.

Cooperation with the police is unlikely in many urban communities where law enforcement's ability to solve cases is limited and the risk of retaliation is high, especially when suspects and victims are knit together in local kinship and friendship networks. If residents consider a murder to be a justifiable homicide, they are extremely unlikely to cooperate with police, especially when they have nothing to gain. On the other hand, when they think a murder is unjustified, they are more likely to cooperate.

Richard Rosenfeld, Bruce Jacobs, and Richard Wright (2003) found that street criminals are especially vulnerable to street crime themselves because they engage in risky behavior and cannot rely on the police for protection. They argue that snitching is driven by a variety of motives, including fear, greed, revenge, altruism, the need for recognition, and a desire for reduced jail time. In their study, they found that authorities typically offer a deal, such as reduced charges or outright freedom, in exchange for information. But they also discovered other rationales for snitching. Snitches may deny that the information they gave could harm anyone; no one is hurt by false information. They may declare that their victim deserved to be punished or bought down a peg or two. In this way, the snitch neutralizes his own transgression of the code of the street. Snitching can be passive, such as cooperating with the police to bring down a rival or enemy or informing when their refusal would almost certainly lead to long-term confinement, or more active, such as enlisting the authorities or eagerly cooperating in order to secure valuable benefits.

While these dynamics are important, many law enforcement agencies view snitching within the context of crime rather than examining how it is tied to a larger information network. This chapter offers a more comprehensive analysis of the ways information is shared on Lyford Street, especially concerning police cooperation, by situating the discussion within the interaction order of information, retaliation, and retribution within this community. Outsiders, particularly defense attorneys who are aware of these dynamics, use these rules to gauge the guilt and innocence of clients by understanding the use of information about criminal cases in local disputes. All too often, law enforcement officials regard gossip and hearsay as largely related to motives and typically use them to identify suspects for high-profile crimes. Those who would benefit from providing law enforcement and prosecutors with misinformation in return for a lighter sentence are equally aware of the types of accounts that law enforcement find believable; crimes related to drug dealing and gangs tend to garner more support than accounts about interpersonal deputes.

Seniors and gainfully employed homeowners tend to appeal to law enforcement more often than others do. They have no problem calling the police but are hesitant to cooperate without knowing the facts (Tyler 2004; Rose and Clear 2004). People recounted calling the police to report loiterers or fights near their property. A neighborhood patrol officer was placed in the Lyford Street area largely as a result of the high volume of police calls. When this officer conducted an informal survey of crime, the most frequent complaint was not violence but property crimes such as breaking and entering or robbery. In my research, I heard the same pattern of complaints.

I surmised from the residents' accounts that these crimes were likely to go unsolved, shifting the responsibility to the residents themselves. In practice, they were in charge of handling these crimes, especially once they found out the identity of the wrongdoers. One such incident involved Mr. John, who confronted a new resident about her eight-year-old son, who threw rocks and broke a window. Several residents told Mr. John who did it. Initially, the mother refused to take responsibility after her son denied breaking the window. But when a neighbor urged her to pay for the window, especially since she was new and would need the community to "look out" for her and her family, she complied. The importance of having allies who protect one another's property and children is often overlooked in examinations of community networks. This is a form of social capital within a system of collective efficacy. Information of this sort is crucial to the safety of long-term residents.

Outsiders on Lyford Street

A number of outsiders have come to understand the interaction order of crime in the Lyford Street neighborhood through steady contact over the years. Among those who helpfully explained the code of this street were defense attorneys, teachers and school administrators, local church officials, social workers, patrol officers, and individuals who worked in the juvenile justice system. All of them seemed to have a good sense of the types of crimes plaguing the community and how crime works in these spaces.

Missionaries living in or near Lyford Street since the early 1980s who had never been victims of violence had learned how long-term residents without familial connections could stay safe. While they recognized their outsider status, they knew the neighborhood well enough to avoid places and times where crime and violence were likely to occur. They also understood the difference between crimes related to the drug trade and those that were part of larger interpersonal disputes. Stacy, the white woman who worked with Global Ministries, continued to rely on the neighborhood patrol officer, whom she trusted, even after she had been withdrawn from the beat. "I miss her," Stacy said. "She was the only legit officer." When confronting a situation that she did not know how to handle, Stacy contacted her instead of dialing 911. "One time we found drugs at our house, in the garden," she recalled. "It was a brick of white powder . . . solid," which was worth a fortune. So Stacy called the former patrolwoman, who promised to get it taken care of right away. "Another officer called back and said, 'Don't go outside. Stay in your house until we get there. Don't come outside.' They came in their unmarked cars, undercover. He calls me, like, 'Where is it?' I'm like, 'OK, you're parked.' He's like, 'You're watching me out the window?' I'm like, 'Yeah. Heck, yeah, I'm watching this go down!'" Stacy was laughing, but she understood that law enforcement officers must avoid implicating the missionaries in their confiscation of huge quantities of drugs.

While these outsiders know that their status confers some protection by law enforcement agencies, they are well aware that stray bullets are an ever-present threat. Their interactions with residents tended to be bracketed;

they engaged in church-sponsored after-school programs, criminal defense cases, arrests, and the juvenile justice system. These interactions taught them how to navigate the space and understand the networks of people who live in this community. A skilled and experienced defense attorney who represents clients from Lyford Street and places like it can easily decipher a client's guilt or innocence on the basis of recognizable patterns in violent crimes.

One knowledgeable defense attorney saved a man from serving life in prison. The importance of information is crucial in regard to cold cases. Information is often used as a bargaining tool for those seeking lighter sentences. The use of false information almost landed a man in prison after a female assailant implicated her ex-boyfriend for a lighter sentence.

A female resident of the Lyford Street neighborhood who was on probation assaulted another resident with a knife at a local convenience store. Faced with the possibility of a twenty-year prison stint, this woman produced an account of an unsolved murder case involving a nonresident in exchange for a lighter sentence that would essentially extend her probation. She identified her ex-boyfriend as the shooter in the murder and agreed to testify against him. As a part of her plea bargain, she would be relocated from Lyford Street and placed in protective custody.

In court, this witness testified that she saw her ex-boyfriend murder the outsider. Her house was located on the same street, but more than ten houses away from where the crime occurred. Her ex-boyfriend was arrested and charged on the basis of her report. What made her account convincing was that it had all the right elements: she stated that he was a drug dealer, part of a gang on Lyford Street, and extremely violent, and she feared for her safety.

The ex-boyfriend's defense attorney not only had a good sense of the drug trade in the Lyford Street community but was aware of insider accounts of the actual circumstances surrounding the murder, which he obtained through gossip from highly credible sources. While this attorney was certain that his client was innocent, proving it was a challenge since no other arrest was made in the case. His job was to discredit the witness and point out the implausibility of the crime. His client, who was neither a local resident nor a Lyford Street drug dealer, took the arrest as a blessing; he hoped to sue the city for wrongful arrest and imprisonment. This attorney cautioned his client not to sabotage his case by refusing to cooperate; there was a high probability that a jury would find him guilty on the basis of his ex-girlfriend's account, so he could spend the rest of his life in prison.

The slippery slope for the attorney was that he, like a number of residents on Lyford Street, knew that the murder of this prominent outsider was due to an interpersonal dispute, not drug dealing or gangs. His first job was to discredit the witness, which was not difficult given her criminal record. Moreover, at the time of the murder her electronic monitoring device placed her at home, not on the street in the vicinity of the crime. Her subsequent conduct also tended to discredit her, as she became pregnant by an officer assigned to her case while in protective custody. Crucially, this attorney understood how residents used law enforcement and state agencies to retaliate against each other. His client's case lacked the recognizable factors of retaliation related to the drug trade: his client was twenty-eight at the time—too old to be a street dealer—and he had very little knowledge about the Lyford Street community and no motive to murder a man he did not know. Instead, the attorney realized, this case was related to a relationship that had ended badly and a woman who was trying to save herself from going to prison. He also understood the incentives in the plea-bargaining process. Most important, he could avail himself of high-quality gossip from credible informants who told him what had actually happened and whose accounts corroborated one another.

While the witness's ex-boyfriend was found innocent, the accuser proved to be an embarrassment for the state. Several thousand dollars were spent for her protective custody, including an apartment for more than a year, and she was released on probation rather than being sent to prison.

Cat and Mouse: Exposing Lies and Falsehoods

A "cat and mouse" strategy involves outing an untrustworthy person and places the burden on whoever receives information to correct misinformation or disinformation. Dealers in the neighborhood use this strategy to identify liars and stigmatize the untrustworthy. While many residents looked up my personal background online and asked me questions to see whether I would lie, one of my main informants set up an elaborate test not only to confirm my identity but also to ascertain whether, if told a false story where we both shared assumed similar information, I would do the honorable thing and tell the truth. I passed the test, but it also put my safety at risk.

Fred, a neighborhood resident and drug user, became one of my most trusted and important participants in the study, and he introduced me to Dave, his dealer. Dave grew up in Bristol Hill and even worked the corner briefly on Lyford Street. He was a successful independent dealer who had never been caught in his seventeen years in the trade. I was impressed that Dave transitioned Fred from hard drugs such as heroin, freebase cocaine, and, later, crack cocaine to marijuana and provided Fred with cocaine only sporadically to prevent him from relapsing. The two men had a father-son relationship.

I met Dave at a suburban gym where he and Fred worked out together once a week. When we first met, I told him that I was a sociologist and that my work in Bristol Hill involved serving as an expert witness in a case he was very familiar with. It took six months before he would agree to talk to me about growing up in Bristol Hill and another three months before he would tell me anything about the drug trade.

Nine months later, after working out, we decided to go back to Fred's place to try Dave's new brand of marijuana, which he saved for friends. I wanted to interview Dave mostly because he knew the politics of the drug trade, but he was also very well read, especially in black history. We often discussed social theory, religion, and our families, but we rarely discussed the drug trade in Bristol Hill. Going to Fred's place to watch them smoke marijuana seemed a natural way for me to introduce the topic while building trust and rapport.

Dave showed us his new variety of marijuana, which he stored in small green transparent plastic boxes. Each box sold for twenty-five dollars, but this box was for sampling. As Dave lit up a blunt, I lit a cigarette, which he hated because he despised the smell of burning tobacco. We debated about whether cigarettes were worse than marijuana, but agreed to disagree. So while Dave and Fred smoked marijuana, I smoked my cigarette. We were also drinking Hennessey, which lightened the mood. Then I was presented with a threat steeped in misinformation.

Dave said that he believed the receptionist at the gym was an undercover drug enforcement agent. This man, a Puerto Rican in his late twenties, had worked at the gym for less than a year. The gym, located at least twenty minutes away from the city and whose patrons were mostly white and middle-class, seemed an odd place to investigate the drug trade in Bristol Hill. Dave said, "You know what, I don't trust that nigga Javier; he always asking questions about where he can buy weed. I heard that he was sent here from Miami as a DEA agent. If he keeps asking questions, he's going to find himself dead in a ditch."

Initially, I did not recognize this declaration as a threat directed against me, although I, too, had been asking questions about the drug trade. I was fairly certain that Javier was not a dealer. So, fearing for Javier's safety, I tried to point out why this theory was ridiculous. I blurted out:

> That is the most ridiculous shit I've ever heard. I'm not saying you're wrong, but Javier is not a cop! First, he tried to sell me and Fred steroids in the locker

room; I'm sure that's why the gym posts a sign against the dangers of steroids. Second, he's from Rosedale, a Puerto Rican neighborhood located right outside Bristol Hill; I overheard him telling someone he grew up there. Third, I once got lost when I first started coming to the gym, and he gave me directions via bus routes, meaning he doesn't own a car. Fourth, he has a ponytail with baby hair trimmed and greased up on the side of his head; I'm not saying that he not hood, but that's not a hood haircut. Last, how sad would it be to be sent from Miami to some cold, bland, insecure, middle-class suburb with steroid abusers? Also, he's not the sharpest tool in the shed. Although I've rarely spoken to him, every time I've asked him a question, he always responded, "I don't know; let me find out." You work here! How is it possible you don't know where the trash cans are or the price of a bottle of water? And last, how does one work at a gym, sell steroids, and be mildly obese? I could be wrong, but if he's cop, the standards of law enforcement must be really low. Or, who knows, maybe he's there to take down a steroid ring of insecure men with exaggerated bodies. How sad would that be?

While I was saying all that, Fred and Dave were laughing so hard that they began to tear up. Two hours later, Dave drove me back to my car at the gym and agreed to be interviewed about growing up in Bristol Hill. It wasn't until a few weeks later that Fred told me the threat was directed toward me: if I turned out to be a cop, I would end up in a ditch. The degree of trust involved in acting like his friend, sitting at his table, and meeting members of his family meant that Dave needed me to know that if I betrayed him there would be consequences. In telling the story about Javier, Dave was trying to gauge my response to see both whether I might be an undercover police officer and whether I would lie, knowing that we shared similar experiences with Javier. I passed the test because instead of accepting Dave's account, I pointed out its implausibility.

Since as an ethnographer I ask questions very similar to those posed by police investigators, our informal interviews made Dave uncomfortable. Once he even showed up with his girlfriend at the community college where I worked to see whether I was telling the truth about my job. Fred said that Dave genuinely liked me, however, and we began to spend time together without Fred. Dave soon became one of my most valued sources of information, and I considered him a friend. In many ways Fred protected me by vouching for my credibility; indeed, without him I would have been unable to complete this research.

Roger Gould (2003) pointed out that violent conflict is likely to occur in symmetrical relationships among friends and within families. With regard to retaliation, he emphasized that violence tends to be local and that violence in places like Bristol Hill has an order to it that seems to be defined by the rules of those in the know. In the Lyford Street community, there are very few anonymous actors. Tracing the source of information leaks requires the reproduction of an account with details that only a witness or someone who heard their testimony could produce.

The Patrol Officer's Perspective

During my time in the field I worked with an experienced neighborhood patrol officer who was assigned to Lyford Street under a federal grant. A native of Bristol Hill, she had witnessed the changes in the drug trade from the early 1980s. Although she did not grow up on Lyford Street, she had a cousin who moved to the neighborhood around the same time she joined the police force.

We were first introduced while I was volunteering at a neighborhood community outreach organization, when she ran my background check. Once she followed up on my references, she announced that I would be working mainly with her, including participating in her neighborhood patrols. Our relationship for the first few months was extremely tense. She had voiced her concern that academics were naive and said that, although she did not personally like my work on Jonathan's case and my interest in drug dealing, she was going to show me the truth. It took more than six months for us to become friendly, sharing stories about our families and the role of education in our upward mobility. We had many heated exchanges. We disagreed most fundamentally on the role of law enforcement, whether it was a good idea to demolish vacant properties, methods of fund-raising, and the future of the community.

Our arguments usually concerned what sort of sanctions would help solve the neighborhood's problems. Three issues were particularly contentious during the early months of our acquaintance. The first involved ticketing residents for the poor upkeep of their houses. I argued that because so many residents were renters and not homeowners, fining them would not improve the appearance of the neighborhood. Neighborhood cleanups were organized by the agency where we both worked. The compromise was identifying owners who were not maintaining the properties through code enforcement.

Our second contentious exchange related to defining the needs of the community. The community service agency that employed us was influential in deciding what the residents needed; the people were given no opportunity to decide for themselves. The agency received a $50,000 grant for neighborhood beautification. I sided with the residents, stating that they should have been asked what they wanted instead of being given what the agency wanted. The patrol officer felt that the money had to be spent and that if residents were given the money directly, it was very unlikely that it would be used on repairs. Ultimately, owner-occupied residences received streetlights and new fences, and the remaining funds were used for supplies for neighborhood cleanups and block-party-style barbeques as a reward.

Our last, and most challenging, dispute had to do with viable solutions to the serious problems posed by the drug trade. We agreed that employment opportunities and improved education were needed, but I thought that arresting large numbers of teenage boys and sending them to juvenile facilities for drug crimes was not curbing the trade (Clear 2007). She argued that it was her job to uphold the law and that my critique of arresting offenders was not a solution to the problem.

Despite these ongoing arguments, the police officer and I developed a healthy degree of a mutual respect. Her job involved serving as a community liaison, identifying the needs of residents, and presenting their grievances to the police force and government funders. Most of our activities involved working with children, including weekly trips to a city swimming pool for local day camps, as well as neighborhood cleanups and barbeques. She patrolled the neighborhood from 9:00 a.m. to 5:00 p.m., with community activities built in throughout the day. Her position was unique because she rarely arrested people in the neighborhood; instead, she would covertly arrange for other officers who were on patrols in different parts of town to make arrests, especially those involving kids in the drug trade.

Her knowledge of the neighborhood made her aware of where most of the dealers lived, as well as their family circumstances. She built trusting relationships with residents who sought her help in neighborhood disputes. She knew many of the long-term residents, particularly the parents of children we transported to the park or pool. People viewed her as a valuable resource for formal and informal solutions to their problems, not as an outsider who interfered with their lives (Tyler 2004; Rose and Clear 2004). Her networks were extremely helpful to me in identifying long-term residents to interview. She not only vouched for my reputation but personally introduced me to many of the homeowners who were a part of this study. In essence, her goal of making sure that my narrative was well informed opened up networks I was not initially exposed to. She once told me: "You need to speak to as many people as possible. There are families who have lived here all their life; they will tell you one story. They're people who just moved here; they will tell you another. They're people who work here, and they will tell you another story. People who stay here stay here because they have family, and that counts for a lot. I watched those boys grow up; our families know each other." The officer knew that I had volunteered on a major drug case. She tended to empathize with the people in the neighborhood, and I respected that her job had a clear protocol defining what she was required to do when she witnessed a crime. Despite our initial disagreements over policy, we eventually looked to each other for advice.

Her creative policing was based on her intimate acquaintance with community networks. For example, she encountered a fairly new eighteen-year-old independent dealer who owed $5,000 to his supplier after a robbery that included a sizable amount of drugs and who faced a legal case that proved especially costly because of a probation violation. If drugs that have been supplied to a dealer on credit are stolen or confiscated, the debt must nonetheless be paid, and it accumulates interest. This dealer and his family feared that his life and their home would be in danger if he failed to come up with the money he owed. In an effort to save her son's life, the mother went to Mr. John for help. I was present when the patrol officer and Mr. John arranged for the temporary arrest of the dealer, keeping him and his family out of harm's way until they came up with the money. The supplier, who was based out of state, apparently made a threat that both the dealer's family and the police took very seriously.

The strategic actions of the parents, residents, and patrol officer focused on working within neighborhood networks, and Mr. John's association with the patrol officer played a large part in the solution. I initially heard this account from the officer, but on another occasion Mr. John told me that the mother was a close friend of his and looked out for his house. She was aware of Mr. John's relationship with the officer (his son was a police officer as well), but, most importantly, Mr. John was known for coming up with viable solutions to problems. Mr. John understood how this community works and could suggest an alternative approach to situations that direct police intervention could not resolve—and might have ended in death.

Teenagers' Hot Spot Networks

One of the greatest challenges of this ethnography in Bristol Hill was keeping in contact with those residents who tended to move from house to house and change their phone numbers frequently. While volunteering in after-school programs that offered free Wi-Fi hot spots—spaces to access the Internet at no cost—I noticed that many teens with smartphones and music devices were using the hot spots to communicate with one another using social media.

Many social networking programs have filters enabling users to limit who can see the information they post. Many teens reported that they relied on such privacy features to create a buffer from parents who aimed to monitor their communications. With the rise of smartphones and iPods and the availability of free Wi-Fi services, these systems became one of the primary ways that teens in Bristol Hill communicated with one another.

A number of flash mobs developed while I was in the field: a group of people would unexpectedly assemble in a particular space and do something to attract attention. I was not interested in this phenomenon until I became aware that a birthday party for a seventh-grade girl, at which the parents were expecting about fifteen kids, turned into a gathering of more than a hundred people after the invitation was re-sent over social media. While I was struck by the fact that more than a hundred teens had free time on a Saturday afternoon, the mother of the teenage girl was curious to know how people found out about the party. We later learned that a combination of texting, Facebook, tweets, and Instagram messages spread the word. These networks also offered a particular form of capital, with teens who viewed themselves as popular boasting about their number of "followers." A teen with hundreds of followers can easily draw a crowd to an event.

Many teens tweeted about their personal lives, especially whom they were dating, but they also used social media to spread gossip. Knowing that phone service was costly, few parents suspected the density of communication between their children and their peers. And since proximity to a hot spot was required, many parents without Internet access did not witness their children using these devices. Despite their dire financial straits, teens were able to pass along information using social networks, finding a way to send text messages using services that defied cell phone companies' control. Most importantly, teens kept their activities private from their parents while publicizing them widely among their peers. Young adults' sophisticated use of social media is an often overlooked form of collective efficacy that drastically impacts the diffusion and spread of information within youth networks. The use of social media shapes the interaction order with regard to information, but it is also an important feature of gossip networks.

Making Sense of Gossip

To understand crimes of violence in this community, we must examine residents' relationships with both one another and the state. People in close-knit communities tend to rely on one another in case of conflict. Issues of credibility, gossip, snitching, and trust are vitally important. Gossip relies heavily on both negative and positive forms of credibility. Unlike snitching, which depends primarily on witnessing and being part of an event with particular rewards and sanctions, gossip has a way of maintaining solidarity by sharing crucial information. An interaction-order approach to gossip shows its collective efficacy: it helps keep people safe and makes life more manageable for those in the know.

The role of the gossip requires a certain amount of informational reciprocity; credible gossip must be recognizable and likely to be true. While gossip requires a certain level of involvement, it can be speculative and based on hearsay. A well-connected member of the community in multiple gossip networks who may or may not have access to those who witnessed a specific set of events may be able to shape an account that can be taken as accurate, or at least credible. Gossip also serves as a way of correcting misinformation circulating in the network.

Snitching is shaped by both insiders and outsiders, as incentives to cooperate by informing on criminals require the production of an account that implicates individuals who participated in or witnessed particular events. Residents who are facing criminal charges may produce the right type of information for law enforcement, including forms of gossip and hearsay that violate taken-for-granted notions of witnessing and participation. This analysis gives insight into snitching, gossip, retaliation, and retribution with regard to drug dealing and murders that are solved and those types of crimes that are likely to go unsolved.

The line between gossip and snitching is razor thin, especially when law enforcement agencies ask residents to cooperate by recounting events that they did not witness but know about only through hearsay. Moreover, law enforcement officials rarely consider the implications of these practices for networks that are essential for poor communities. As members of a socially marginalized group, impoverished black people realize that their ability to obtain justice is limited by race and class. Within the neighborhood, justice is initially administered locally. People without societal support who are estranged from the state and disconnected from the larger economy do not expect law enforcement to help them. This point is driven home when crimes against outsiders are disproportionately investigated and solved but crimes among insiders are ignored. Indeed, as the war on drugs, housing policy, and welfare and education reform show, the state is more punitive than protective. Knowing one another and the rules that prevail within the community is essential.

Being connected to the information networks within this community allows people to live in relative safety, even when they are forced to use what Elijah Anderson (2000) calls street justice. Here, the local order collides with the criminal justice system. This situation is further blurred when the media report on the tactics of the criminal justice system and then interview from that biased standpoint, creating an account that is based on information that is not entirely true. As Albert J. Meehan (2000) found in Oakland, California, a gang narrative is constructed not only by the media but also by the various legal and political bodies that must account for illegal behavior.

Given the differences between gossip and snitching, as well as the variations between insider and outsider accounts, I decided to examine residents' accounts of how murder happens in this community. The predictable patterns I discovered provide them with the knowledge they need to stay safe in dangerous situations, but this understanding of life around them is obscured by outsiders' accounts. This gap not only creates misinformation but also generates pervasive mistrust of outsiders. When the area where the crime occurred is economically depressed, heavily impoverished, drug infested, and politically marginalized, a gang narrative becomes quite believable. Outsiders who produce an account specific to their enterprise— police records, court indictments, and newspaper stories—usually present instances of law breaking as disorderly events. In local everyday life, however, violence is anything but disorder: it is often predictable and based on reasons that locals understand.

FIVE

The Politics of Murder and Revenge

Mr. John, a sixty-five-year-old long-term resident, described the social distance that exempted outsiders such as myself from violence and the interpersonal grievances that precipitated violence among insiders.

> They're not gonna mess with you. Somebody white coming here, they're not gonna mess with them. They mess with each other. That's the shameful part. You know, they shouldn't mess with anybody, but they do. They mess with each other. And it's crazy. You could come through here three, four o'clock in the morning; they're not gonna mess with you. But that nineteen-year-old guy who they called their buddy last week, they'll get with him if they feel as though he wronged them. Or that little black guy from across town, they feel as though he's wrong. That's who they get with. And that's what it is.

This distinction rang true as I came to learn more about the instances of personal violence that had involved Jonathan and other members of the Lyford Street community. My involvements in Jonathan's death-penalty case led me to interrogate the orderliness of neighborhood violence and interpersonal disputes.

The intimate character of interpersonal conflict arises from the fact that Bristol Hill is remarkably stable. Before the introduction of charter schools, most of the children attended the same elementary school, middle school, and high school. By my rough estimate, at least a quarter of the residents are related as distant cousins and through intermarriage and parenthood. Most are familiar with one another; many know one another well. Although crime is a far too common occurrence in the neighborhood, murder is rare. The five murders in the neighborhood, four of which remain unsolved, exemplify the ways in which the local interaction order shapes the narrative surrounding the motives for the murders.

Guns, like drug dealing, are part of everyday life in Bristol Hill. Yet law enforcement and the media only showed interest in the murders when a prominent citizen who was not from the neighborhood was killed. Police and prosecutors constructed a drug-gang narrative to connect these crimes to suspects who could be prosecuted. The five murders were eventually prosecuted in three separate cases in different court systems. The accused and the cooperating witnesses were all living in the neighborhood; some were involved in drug dealing along Lyford Street. Residents and local police officers were certain that no gangs were operating in the area. Yet according to the local media, police records, and prosecutors' indictments, members of drug gangs committed all of the murders.

When murder, which is relatively rare in most communities, is interpreted by people from outside the neighborhood, they tend to project their own preconceptions upon it. Prosecutors commonly put forward the notion that deadly violence is gang related because they regard inner-city neighborhoods as pathological. The gang narrative serves to explain the inexplicable, especially if this narrative goes unchallenged in the justice system. Residents, in contrast, consistently disputed the gang narrative and articulated their own locally embedded accounts that focused on relationships between individuals and the local social code. They pointed toward motives and reasons that everyone who lived there understood, including self-defense, revenge, economic gain, and the desire to avoid a long prison sentence (Katz 2008; Collins 2009). The murders in Bristol Hill were committed for many different reasons, but they all made sense to residents.

I tell the stories of five murders as they were told to me, presenting the overlapping accounts of local residents as they understood the motives of the assailants. One of my main informants was a former drug dealer who helped me interpret my field notes and observations. Most of the other informants were in a position to observe and interpret the events around these murders. These narratives, which articulate local perspectives on these events, contradict the gang narrative put forward by the prosecutors in the criminal cases. By examining the circumstances of each murder, I came to understand certain motivations for these killings that rest on their situated meanings within the local interaction order.

When I asked Mr. John about allegations that these murders were committed by a local drug gang, he responded:

> The Lyford Street Gang? I didn't know anything about the Lyford Street Gang. And I live right here, but I didn't know anything about the Lyford Street Gang, 'cause it just them little bunch of knuckleheads that I always walk past, say,

"Hey, Mr. John." And I [say to them], "Yo," and keep right on going. Just the way it is. . . . I watched these boys grow up. Most of them grow up, you know. And that's the thing, you see the change, but you still see the little boy.

Mr. John's narrative captures the sentiment of many residents that these dealers and later "gang members" were kids who grew up in this community. While he recognized that many have changed, he still sees the little boy inside of them. His account demonstrates how residents who live in Lyford Street are simultaneously aware and unaware of the drug trade, a form of civil inattention that allows residents to remain safe but also blind to the specific details of the drug trade (Goffman 1971).

A Son Kills His Mother's Boyfriend

The story of the so-called Lyford Street Gang began with the murder of a prominent government official I call Leslie. Although this situation was known differently by local residents, the police created the narrative of the Lyford Street Gang to account for his murder. The framing of this murder is significant in relation to the drug trade: dealers, who fear retaliation, go to great lengths not to harm public officials because they assume that police take those murders more seriously than other murders within the neighborhood. The added attention from police tends to disrupt the drug trade, which also made this case stand out.

Leslie, a forty-three-year-old man, was killed by his girlfriend's sixteen-year-old son, Blake, in an altercation concerning his relationship with the boy's mother, thirty-five-year-old Donna. The previous day, Donna had attempted to end her two-year relationship with Leslie. Neighbors overheard their argument and reported the verbal confrontation to police. Donna told her son that when she told Leslie she wanted to break up with him, he hit her. The shooting took place around nine the next evening. That day, Leslie was seen knocking on the door of the home where Donna lived with Blake and his older sister. Later, Leslie's body was found in front of his car a few feet away from Donna's house. Before his death, Leslie left Donna a letter asking her to reconcile, which she later turned over to the police. According to Blake's sister, her younger brother viewed himself as the man of the house and the protector of his mother and sister.

Donna rejected Leslie because she was interested in pursuing a relationship with another man. She was sexually linked to an elected official who was in a position to influence Blake's initial hearing when he was arrested for Leslie's murder. Despite his relationship with Blake's mother, the official used his influence against Blake. Documentation of this affair and DNA evidence linking Donna to both Leslie and the elected official were entered into evidence; a pair of Donna's underwear found in Leslie's car after his death contained her DNA, Leslie's, and that of the elected official. But her relationship with the public official was never discussed during the trial by either the defense or the prosecution.

As I interviewed a number of the attorneys and witnesses involved in this case, it became clear that the attorneys had relationships with one another, the elected official, and friends of Leslie. Most of the defense and prosecuting attorneys and judges had career-long acquaintanceships; public defenders and prosecutors had been mentored by judges in that jurisdiction. Most of the court officers lived in the same community.

Several attorneys said that helping anyone who is accused of murdering an important outsider is difficult. Outsider status is given to anyone who does business on behalf of the state, such as politicians, mail carriers, social workers, law enforcement, trash collectors, teachers, firefighters, and emergency medical technicians. These individuals have a special status because their jobs require them to enter communities where they do not reside. These cases are well attended, and officers work closely with prosecutors to solve them.

Police explained Leslie's murder as the result of the putative Lyford Street Gang's effort to protect its territory and its members' alleged determination to silence anyone who threatened the neighborhood drug enterprise. For instance, if a postal worker delivered mail in a drug hot spot, he or she could easily be used as a witness. Outsiders, myself included, routinely observe illegal activity. Being skilled at turning a blind eye to suspected drug dealing is crucial to maintaining personal safety. If a person's job places him or her at risk, a drug-gang narrative may explain why. This argument, presented by the prosecutors in two other murder trials, described a deadly gang that went to great lengths to punish anyone, including potential witnesses, who challenged the drug enterprise.

From both my interviews with local residents and the official court records, I found no evidence that Blake had ever sold drugs. He and his mother merely lived on Lyford Street. Nevertheless, Leslie's death led to the formation of a seven-agency task force that searched and subpoenaed four hundred residents of the Lyford Street neighborhood under a blanket order intended to protect witnesses from being targets of revenge.

Four Prior Murders and the Genesis of a Gang Narrative

Before Leslie's death, four unsolved murders were on the books. Until Leslie's death there had been no suggestion that any of these deaths were gang related. Soon after his murder, however, a series of legal indictments and media reports began referring to the drug dealers on Lyford Street as the Lyford Street Boys, the Bristol Hill Boys, the Bristol City Crew, and then simply the Lyford Street Gang, which stuck when the county newspaper picked it up.

Jonathan's death-penalty case became my entry point into the neighborhood drug gang narrative. The six drug dealers who were alleged to compose the gang—Jonathan, Antonio, Byron, Joseph, Antoine, and Paul—were charged under a federal law enacted to control organized crime. The prosecutor alleged that the pattern of their actions demonstrated that they belonged to an "ongoing criminal organization." All six were born and lived on Lyford Street. They were closely related through kinship or long-term friendships. To outsiders, then, the gang narrative seemed plausible.

The role of media in naming alleged street gangs has been noted by others (Yablonsky 1959). The reporter from the township newspaper wrote stories about Lyford Street on the basis of information from the indictment, the murder trials, and interviews with the families of the murder victims. In these reports, neither community residents nor local police spoke of the accused as gang members. In court, the drug dealers who were witnesses for the prosecution and were not accused of membership in the gang referred to themselves as "the team" or "the group." None of the accused men was found guilty of racketeering.

Prior to my involvement in Jonathan's case, there were a number of unsolved and high-profile murders. In one of the four murders, four days before Leslie was killed, Janet, a thirty-one-year-old woman who had lived on Lyford Street for twenty years, was shot twice in the back of the head as she was returning from an errand at a neighborhood convenience store in the middle of the afternoon. Her body was found on her front lawn. Her mother, who lived a few blocks away, had picked up Janet's five-year-old daughter before she returned. Just before her death, Janet told her friends and neighbors about a pending court case in which she had been charged with illegally purchasing guns for neighborhood drug dealers. Several of her friends and neighbors were keeping a close watch on her and her daughter because of the case. A witness named Karen, one of Janet's friends, testified that she saw Antoine kill Janet. Karen knew Antoine, a twenty-year-old dealer from the neighborhood, and she also knew that Janet had purchased a gun for him.

Janet had grown up with all the guys in the neighborhood; their families were well acquainted. Janet was a second cousin to two of the accused, Antonio and Jonathan. It had been her practice to take drug dealers to the gun shop. They would choose a gun, and she would purchase it using their money. She had bought seven guns this way for five different dealers.

Two men were arrested with guns in their possession that Janet had purchased. One was Antonio, whose brother, Jonathan, was the accused whose defense began my involvement with this neighborhood. The other was a nineteen-year-old named Joseph. Five guns that were traced back to Janet remained missing. In return for her testimony against those for whom she had illegally obtained weapons, Janet would have received three years' probation, and whomever she testified against would have received a three-year prison term. Janet told authorities that she was going to testify only against Antonio, who was already in jail at the time of the initial charges. But she needed to produce the other weapons to convince the police that Antonio was the only person she had given guns to. She wanted Antonio and Jonathan to help her get the remaining guns back from the other three men who had them—Joseph, Paul, and Antoine—so that she would not have to testify against all of the parties involved.

Janet wanted to pin all the gun purchases on Antonio because he was an easy fall guy. During my interviews with members of his family, even before they knew about his IQ test results, they described Antonio as nice but "intellectually challenged." His sister described him as "not that bright but a hard worker." His mother agreed. His father said that Antonio was his favorite child because he always did what he asked him to do. Antonio had been diagnosed as mentally retarded while in elementary school and later was tested by psychologists; he scored in the "mentally retarded" range twice and just two points above it once. His name on the street was Watermelon Head. As he got older, people called him Melo, short for "melon," a put-down that referred to his gullibility.

Janet told Antonio that she was going to testify against him. When Janet's mother found out about the gun case, she spoke to Jonathan and Antonio, who assured her that Janet would be safe. Janet's mother was also told about the plan to get the guns back. According to Paul, a twenty-year-old dealer and former resident of Lyford Street who was one of the other gun owners and testified during an unrelated drug trial, Janet had told him that she was going to tell the prosecutor that the other five guns she had previously purchased and were unaccounted for all belonged to Antonio. She also told her story to anyone else who would listen, including at least seven other people in addition to her two second cousins. Apparently, she believed that talking to so many people would ensure her safety, because all the parties involved had been named and they would be suspects if something happened to her. She joked about "wearing a wire" to record her conversations secretly on behalf of the police, telling various people in the neighborhood that if she were wearing a wire she would give them a signal to let them know.

Janet's murder was still being investigated when Leslie was killed. Blake, who was arrested for the murder of his mother's boyfriend, was tied to the so-called Lyford Street Gang primarily because the gun he used to kill Leslie had been purchased by Janet. Janet had not bought this gun for Blake, however; she had bought it for Joseph, another local dealer. Many of the guns used by the dealers on Lyford Street are stashed near the corner. It was common for dealers working the corner to share guns as a form of protection, but the practice of keeping a gun near the corner rather than carrying a weapon is also way for dealers to avoid weapons charges for possession of a firearm. Blake borrowed the gun from a vacant house used to store weapons and drugs on Lyford Street. After the murder, Blake returned the gun to one of the usual hiding places.

Immediately after Karen witnessed Janet's murder, she called the police, identified the murderer as Antoine, and went into hiding in a neighboring state. Antoine was later arrested; he confessed to Janet's murder and told Paul that he "shot her twice and put her brains to the side of the car for fucking with [his] money." He agreed to testify against Jonathan, Antonio, Byron, and Joseph. For his cooperation, he received a twenty-year sentence for murdering Janet.

Antoine testified that Antonio and Jonathan had ordered him to kill Janet. Both men were home at the time of her murder, and Antonio was under house arrest and wearing an electronic monitoring device. Antonio and Jonathan, who were also Janet's cousins, were later charged with conspiracy to commit murder. Previously, they had been charged only with the sale and possession of cocaine. Similar charges were filed against Byron, Joseph's cousin and Jonathan's childhood friend.

Antoine's cooperation with prosecutors extended to testimony in two other murders. Darnell, a neighborhood acquaintance, was murdered over a dice game. Omar, the stepfather of Jonathan's daughter Violet and father of Violet's year-old half-sister, was also murdered. In addition, Omar shot his own cousin, John. Antoine also admitted to being present at the murder of Thomas, a drug dealer who was killed because he was suspected of cooperating with the police. These men were all competitors on the corner. Although they had grown up in the neighborhood and a few of them had close familial relationships, they were not all friends, let alone a gang.

Revenge: You Killed My Cousin

Omar was murdered at the age of twenty, three years before Leslie's death. Paul, a twenty-year-old Lyford Street resident, drug dealer, and witness for the prosecution, testified that while Omar was in prison on drug charges three months before his death, his thirty-one-year-old girlfriend, Whitney, sold his bulletproof vest and gun to his second cousin on his mother's side, a nineteen-year-old marijuana dealer named John. According to Paul, when Omar was released from prison, he and Omar went to John's home and demanded that he return Omar's gun and vest. John told them that he was not going to give them anything and that he had paid $500 for the gun and vest. John told Omar to see his girlfriend and, finally, said he had already sold the gun and bulletproof vest to someone else.

Paul testified that Omar shot John twice in the chest while standing on his porch. At the time, John had been living with his mother, Catherine. She found her son's body when she returned from work. Catherine knew that her son was a dealer and believed his death was drug related, but she did not know the particulars. When neighbors were questioned by the police, no one was forthcoming. The investigation lasted only two days. After two months, his murder was still unsolved. John's cousin Byron, who was also a neighborhood dealer, began asking questions. A neighbor who was never questioned by police investigators told Byron that he saw Paul and Omar leave the scene of the shooting, and people saw Byron confront Paul and ask him about this incident.

Two months after John's murder, Omar was selling drugs on a corner of Lyford Street when a silver minivan pulled up. It was dark, around 10:00 p.m., and visibility was poor. Someone fired two shots into Omar's chest and then another twelve at close range until the gun was emptied. Although at least thirty people witnessed the shooting and reported hearing the clicks of an empty gun, initially no one was willing to cooperate with law enforcement. A neighbor who lived two houses away from the murder, a sixty-year-old married woman named Mrs. Sanchez, said that once she realized who had been shot, she was somewhat "happy" because of all the "trouble" that Omar had caused over the years, including drug dealing in front of her home and other shootings. After she found out it was him, she took a sleeping pill and kissed her husband good night; she was not going to lose any sleep over Omar.

During the murder investigation, none of the more than four hundred neighborhood residents who were subpoenaed would identify the shooter. Dion, a cocaine addict who lived nearby, later testified that even though visibility was poor, he could identify Byron as the shooter because he knew how Byron moved and recognized him as he was walking toward the body to take the last shots. Dion testified that he "thought" he could identify the driver of the minivan as Jonathan on the basis of his silhouette.

After Paul was arrested on an unrelated drug charge that would have led to a ten-year prison stay unless he cooperated with prosecutors, he voluntarily told police that Byron had killed Omar, his own second cousin, because Omar had killed his cousin John. Although he did not witness the second killing, he said that after Omar's death Byron told him that he had done it. When Paul testified against Omar and Byron, he said that he did not cooperate with the police initially because he feared Omar would kill him. He also testified that he called Byron to let him know when Omar was on the corner alone.

Killed on Suspicion of Snitching

Two years before Leslie was killed, Thomas, a fourteen-year-old dealer, was shot twice in the back of the head. His body was found in a wooded park located in a major city twenty-five miles from Bristol Hill. A police officer who was at the park on his break testified that he heard the gunshots, proceeded toward the sound, and saw a silver 1989 Chevrolet Impala take off. After a pursuit, he found the car abandoned with three doors hanging open, and he heard footsteps and the rustling of branches in the woods. The officer did not pursue on foot but called for backup; a police helicopter and scent-tracking dogs arrived on the scene. Forensic tests found Antoine's fingerprints in the front of the Impala and Antonio's fingerprints in the backseat. Police traced the car to a man named Kenny Mack, who rented it out to people in the Lyford Street neighborhood. Kenny told the authorities that he had rented it to Antoine. When the police interviewed Antoine, he told them he had himself lent the car to Thomas, but the youth had not returned it. Kenny reported the car stolen prior to the police questioning.

About ten days before his murder, Thomas had been arrested along with three other "youngboys," the local term for low-level drug dealers between the ages of twelve and seventeen. Thomas was released a few hours later, while the others each spent three days in jail. When Thomas returned to the corner after staying in the house lying low for a week, the three other youngboys teamed up and jumped him. They were suspicious that Thomas was released so quickly and accused him of being a snitch. The fact that Antoine's drug stash spots were raided after Thomas was arrested also aroused their ire. Antoine, one of the two major drug suppliers to the dealers of Lyford Street, was their boss; Jonathan, the other major supplier, was Thomas's boss. Thomas would have known where Antoine and his youngboys kept their stashes because all the dealers operated in close proximity on the street.

When Jonathan saw Antoine's youngboys ganging up on his youngboy, he intervened, making them fight Thomas one-on-one. After the fight was over, he picked up the bruised and bleeding Thomas and took him home. According to Jonathan, he protected Thomas and put the word out to the other youngboys that no harm was to come to him. This statement was corroborated in court by the three youngboys who had attacked Thomas. Antoine, who turned witness for the prosecution after he was positively identified as Janet's murderer, made a plea deal in exchange for naming Thomas's murderer.

According to Antoine's testimony, he and Antonio picked up Thomas under the guise that they were going to "re-up"—that is, get a new supply of drugs—in the city, but instead Antonio drove to the park and shot Thomas twice in the head. When the police pursued them, Antonio called his brother Jonathan to rescue them. Ultimately, Antonio was convicted of Thomas's murder and sentenced to life in prison. He escaped the death penalty only because of his prior intellectual disability diagnosis. Antoine was never charged, even as an accessory. He was sentenced to twenty years in prison for killing Janet.

According to the police, Thomas did not cooperate with them or inform them of anything, as the other youngboys had believed. He was released early because it was his first arrest. Antoine's drugs were discovered and confiscated based on information supplied by one of his own dealers.

Deadly Dice Game

Darnell was a regular dice player behind Luigi's convenience store. Luigi's is the only store within a two-mile radius of Lyford Street and considered to be a neutral space for dice games attended by drug dealers and other residents. Darnell was twenty-five years old when he was murdered. According to Jonathan, who was eighteen at the time, he lost $5,000 playing dice with Darnell. In this neighborhood, it is customary that when you win all of another man's money, you always give him back 10 percent as "walk-away" money. But when their game was over, Darnell did not give Jonathan his share. Jonathan became angry and brandished a gun. Jonathan, who was younger than Darnell, felt it was crucial for him to command the respect of older men in the community. If he let Darnell get away with this insult, he would lose their respect.

According to Allen Walker, who witnessed this confrontation along with four other players, none of whom ever came forward, Jonathan fired a shot in the air and demanded his 10 percent back. Darnell complied, giving back $500, but the older man was shocked by Jonathan's actions and told him that he was a dead man for having challenged him. Jonathan put his gun away and walked home. Later that day, Darnell stopped at Jonathan's parents' home, where Jonathan no longer lived, apparently looking for him. The following day, a masked man shot Darnell and killed him while he was playing dice at Luigi's. Of the six men who witnessed this shooting, only Allen would testify.

Allen was playing dice with Darnell at the time. During the initial investigation, he said that he didn't know who the shooter was because the man wore a mask. Three years later, when he testified before a grand jury after being charged with violating probation, he changed his statement, testifying on behalf of the prosecution that he knew the masked man was Jonathan based on his gait. Allen and Paul also testified that Darnell had intended to kill Jonathan because of the gun incident, so they saw the murder as a form of self-defense. In exchange for his testimony, Allen received a lesser charge for a pending drug case.

Antoine was the key witness in Darnell's case. He was also present at two of the other murders. The same method, two shots to the head, was used to kill both Janet and Thomas. Janet provided law enforcement with information incriminating Antoine, but her recorded statement was never entered into evidence in the case against Antoine and he was never charged.

The Politics of Murder

Several alleged eyewitnesses of these murder cases, who themselves had pending charges were offered plea deals; some testified in return for lesser sentences, others had their subsidized housing and public assistance continued (a conviction would have meant an eviction), and some of their probation and parole violations went unreported. The degree to which community members cooperated with police in solving these cases varied. Local residents were extremely unlikely to cooperate if they believed the murder to be justifiable homicide, especially when they knew they had nothing to gain through their cooperation. Cooperation is unlikely in many urban communities where the police have open access to information.

Significantly, the story that was produced in the courtroom contradicted what the locals understood to be the truth—and which kept most of them relatively safe from the violence stemming from interpersonal disputes (Collins 2009). Adding to the confusion, the local newspaper published an account that mixed the official and local narratives. This story was initially informed by police records but followed up by interviews with relatives of victims within the context of a pending legal case. Accurate information concerning ongoing interpersonal disputes between known actors allowed residents to steer clear of conflicts that did not involve them (Collins 2009; Katz 2008).

The fact that community members often view killings as acts of justifiable homicide must be acknowledged. Legally, justifiable homicide would not be considered murder if local residents' views prevailed. When the killing is viewed as totally unjustified, individuals in the community are more likely to cooperate with law enforcement. Cooperation with a murder investigation follows a predictable pattern: the justifiability of the murder, consideration of the assailants' motivation, informants' concern for their personal safety, and the likelihood that the police will be able to solve the case are all factored in.

Both classic and contemporary ethnographic studies have explored the social meanings, recruitment processes, and interaction orders of street gangs (Garot 2007; Horowitz 1983; Moore, Garcia, and Garcia 1978, Moore 1985; Short 1974; Thrasher 1927; Venkatesh 1997). Surprisingly few studies, however, have critically examined the process through which law enforcement authorities construct a gang myth as an aid to prosecution in a community where gangs do not exist. Misconstruing crimes as gang violence when there are clear individual motives leads to their description by law enforcement authorities and the media as "senseless" acts of "random violence." In fact, many of these "random" acts of violence are usually tied to interpersonal disputes related to retribution, issues over turf, and harm to innocent bystanders (Collins 2009). In the case of Bristol Hill, the murders turned out to be closely tied to local orders of expectation and practice. They are far from senseless and random—indeed, so much so that people in the community can usually avoid becoming targets and predict who is likely to become a victim. By probing residents' local knowledge and viewpoints, we can see these crimes in contextual and situational terms: these acts are interactional, learned, commonly recognized, temporally ordered, sanctioned, and even rewarded (Garfinkel and Rawls 2006, 2008). The local community on Lyford Street has an order of its own that gives meaning to these events. Participants in social arenas construct coherence in their daily actions and routines through orderly social processes, which in turn form the foundation of their assumptions about the world. Ethnographic knowledge about the orderly properties of different types of social activities within the locality is essential to understanding how and why a particular event or a series of events happens in a specific place and time.

In these five murders, although local residents, drug dealers, and even some local police officers did not consider those accused to be gang members, the gang narrative organized the prosecutions—which meant that the situationally informed motivations behind the murders were not explored. Hence, what actually happened was rendered irrelevant. The interpersonal disputes that gave rise to these actions were never revealed in court, even though they motivated those who falsely informed on others as well as the killers. The gang narrative is an effective tool for prosecutions. In addition, given the many discrepancies between lived accounts and those propagated by the media and the state, residents who were not involved in these cases but were in the know treated these accounts as warnings of what happens when someone becomes involved in the underground economy. Lyford Street residents knew that death was a possibility. They explained that while danger was ever present, they took steps to avoid becoming victims of gun violence: they avoided dealers, stayed close to home, and limited their interactions with those known to be violent, including residents who were not drug dealers.

The Orderliness of Seemingly Random Violence

Although acts of violence in Bristol Hill are typically portrayed by outsiders as senseless, random, and disorderly, they conform to a local order that takes into account the community's economic isolation and the relatively capricious punishments via both street justice and the legal system—which are brought to bear on those who are already in a difficult bind. People who live here must constantly take their immediate and future safety into account. Since their lived daily experiences shape their decisions, they are unlikely to cooperate with law enforcement because of its limited ability to keep them safe.

This situation is equally problematic for law enforcement officers who must contend with a local order in which members of the community selectively cooperate with the police and treat information about crimes as a potential bargaining tool. Many arrests are made in this community, but there is little cooperation on either side. The tensions among local accounts, legal tactics, and media representations add to the misunderstandings. Yet in spite of the problematic relationship between community members and outsiders, witnesses do sometimes come forward to identify killers and then go into hiding until the cases blow over. Equally important, parents go to the men who mean to harm their children and try to negotiate their safety.

The limited, skewed way in which law enforcement investigates and prosecutes these crimes obscures and distorts the local understanding of why murders happen here. This series of cases remained unsolved until the death of an important outsider brought in another set of outsiders who were committed to solving his murder. All lives are valued equally by residents. The creation of a drug-gang narrative may allow for the prosecution of drug dealers as gang members, but it also produces accounts that contradict the evidence regarding these events and ultimately links people together in such a way that they can be prosecuted and convicted unequally and often unjustly. A focus on the meaning and order of the street corner and the neighborhood offers a very different perspective.

In any social situation, participants act in accordance with expectations that are generally taken for granted. The local order of Lyford Street, such as the informal rules governing eye contact, is produced moment by moment and has immediate relevance, affecting the actions of everyone in the community. Like these small gestures and interactions, murders must also be studied in local context, for they are produced through patterned relationships in which violence is predictable. Those who avoid trouble and those who commit serious crimes share understandings that defy the narratives imposed by the authorities for their own purposes.

SIX

Collective Punishment: Black Men's Reflections on Everyday Life in Bristol Hill

The ways in which African American men with limited resources interact within their surroundings demonstrate how low-income residents manage poverty in a terrain of life-altering sanctions. Poverty dynamics are constantly changing, and inequality develops under a new set of conditions in every generation.

This chapter suggests a nuanced way of thinking about poor and working-class African American men. We need to pay close attention to the forces that push these men into poverty and keep them there. These are dynamics over which they have no control. Many men in Bristol Hill are hourly wage workers with relatively low levels of education. In this sense they are part of the growing army of the underemployed and unemployed within the working class. They are the children of working-class and poor black Americans who migrated from the South for better opportunities. But rather than rising into the middle class, they have lost ground in an increasingly competitive global economy. To understand this phenomenon, I examine the accounts of six African American men and demonstrate the complex intersections of family dynamics, inadequate education, unemployment, debt, drug dealing, contact with law enforcement, imprisonment, and criminal records in their lives. Through these narratives, we gain a vivid sense of how chronically debilitating their involvements with major social institutions have been for African American men in Bristol Hill.

This chapter revisits arguments presented by classic and contemporary scholars, particularly Elliot Liebow's (1967) "theory of manly flaws" and "shadow values" arguments, William Julius Wilson's (1987) concept of a "marriageable pool," and Victor Rios's (2011) analysis of the "youth control complex." My purpose is not just to document hardship. By placing the narratives of the men I came to know in the context of their community and by bringing germane theoretical frameworks to bear, I hope that scholars and community leaders alike can begin to envision policy solutions fitted to the men's circumstances and experiences.

Six Life Stories

These six narratives exemplify the range of experiences and perspectives that I observed among the many men in Bristol Hill. These men engaged in the ethnographic process with the understanding that I wanted to tell stories about their lives that crystallized the struggles they faced on a daily basis. These narratives grew out of years of contact, where matters as mundane as the weather and issues as serious as joblessness and interpersonal disputes were regularly discussed. I present several stories of situations I witnessed and was told about by others. Usman, Dave, Fred, Marcus, Justin, and Brent provide unique insights into the challenges facing men in the Lyford Street neighborhood.

Usman

I became acquainted with Usman, who was in his mid-fifties, at a Bristol Hill school board meeting protesting the closure of several schools during the middle of the academic year. I had first met him more than six years earlier, while he was serving time in prison and I went through a teacher training program at a state penitentiary that provided college courses for men who were incarcerated. Upon his release, Usman earned a bachelor's degree in business from a prestigious institution and obtained a job as a paralegal at a small law firm, where he was paid under the table. After two years, he quit when the firm refused to hire him through regular procedures, citing his criminal record as the barrier (Wildeman 2009; Western 2002).

In 2006 the city of Bristol Hill welcomed a new corporation that would hire a total of three hundred new employees. As a part of its deal with the city, which offered it several years of property-tax relief, the company promised that it would make a good-faith effort to hire residents of Bristol Hill. It held a series of job fairs, including more than a dozen in Bristol Hill, and informed every attendee who completed a job application that he or she would be guaranteed an interview. Usman attended one of the fairs and submitted an application. With a bachelor's degree and substantial management experience, he possessed all the qualifications and skills required for the position for which he had applied.

While friends of his were contacted for an interview, he was not. When he called the employer's human resources department to inquire why he was not being interviewed, he was told that it was because he had a criminal record (Pager 2008). Usman pointed out to me that state law requires a written notice of the performance of a background check and verification that his criminal record invalidated him for employment. He contended that because he checked the box on the application indicating that he had a criminal record, his application was not reviewed and a background check was never, in fact, conducted.

Usman proceeded to file a lawsuit in which he argued that the practice of using criminal records in an evaluation of a potential employee's qualifications adversely affects a disproportionate number of African Americans and Muslim African Americans. In his legal brief he charged religious and racial discrimination, based on violation of Title VII of the Civil Rights Act, which states that it is illegal to discriminate against anyone on the basis of race, color, religion, national origin, or sex.

While his assertion that such policies adversely affect African Americans may well be correct, it would be difficult to verify—he would have to show that racial (or religious) discrimination occurred by providing evidence that the employer hired white employees (or non-Islamic employees) with criminal records. Additionally, he would have to prove that all applications with a criminal record were discarded. The burden of proof fell largely upon Usman, making it difficult for him to prevail in this case. A judge would likely agree that an employer had a valid interest in not hiring people with criminal records.

His lawsuit was settled out of court. His case made a valid critique of the barriers that men like him encounter in the job market. The criminalization of impoverished black men, including those who are Muslim, severely hinders their ability to find gainful employment, creating a state of stagnation and stalling the hope of reintegration for ex-convicts who have paid for their crimes. Even with a skill set that is in demand, they are unable to obtain employment that provides them with a living wage.

Dave

Access to marriageable partners in low-income communities is, at best, disproportionate and asymmetrical, given the lack of suitable husbands for eligible women. Measuring the pool of marriageable men, or the "rates of employed civilian men to women of the same race and age group" (Wilson

1987, 83), Wilson ascertained that black women face a severe shortage of potential husbands.

Black men who reside in Bristol Hill have dim employment prospects, many have criminal records, and many are in debt. During my field research, I observed that few of the men I interviewed were single; most were in committed relationships. But almost none were married. These men were in an insoluble predicament; although they had access to a large number of potential mates, their illegal activities made them vulnerable to serious sanctions that could be used by anyone, even intimate partners.

Dave was in precisely that sort of predicament. A working-class resident of Lyford Street, he had a high school diploma and had been employed for more than seven years as a maintenance worker for the same local employer, where he made twelve dollars an hour plus benefits. Dave was a successful drug dealer but had never been arrested and had no criminal record. He argued that he sold drugs to compensate for his low earnings in the above-ground economy.

Dave's case is especially interesting in light of Wilson's (1987) "marriage-able pool" argument. It posits the complete opposite: a situation in which quite a few men are deemed eligible but their shortcomings leave them open to rejection and prevent them from fulfilling their aspiration to form a stable relationship with an intimate partner. During my study, Dave's eight-year romantic relationship ended. After an argument that involved his girlfriend claiming he had cheated on her (an allegation he denied), she called the police and reported his drug-dealing activities. Although law enforcement officials never pursued the case, her betrayal meant a permanent rupture in their relationship. Three weeks after the breakup, I was surprised to learn that he had a new girlfriend, whom he was still seeing a year later.

When I asked Dave about the seriousness of his new relationship, he stressed that he had choices. Dave's perception of his position rested on the belief that competition among African American women for the limited number of available black male partners made him a sought-after commodity. The idea that black women compete for employed men as sexual partners seems like a logical consequence of Wilson's assessment, yet since he made this argument the rising rate of incarceration among black men has left an even deeper void for black women who live in places like Bristol Hill. Dave's perception also assumes that all black women are heterosexual and prefer black men to Latino, Asian, and white men. While numerous women had made sexual advances toward him in the workplace and often flirted with him when he and his former girlfriend went out as a couple, he prided himself on the security that came with being in a committed relationship. He recognized that cheating would complicate his life.

> Well, I ain't gonna say it's easy to cheat. Temptation is what you make it. Like, you can do a lot of things. Females always gonna talk to you. Anytime a girl asks you, "You want some ass?" "No, I'm good." It's a whole thing that when you stop thinking about what you got to gain and worry about what you got to lose, it's kind of easy to fall back, relax. 'Cause ain't no such thing as free pussy, and the minute you hit it, you don't know her psychological makeup. You know what I'm saying? You could fuck her, and she might chill, and y'all might be cool. You call every now and then; do what y'all do or whatever. Or she could just be crazy, fuck around and say that you got her pregnant, or you know what I mean? Just any silly stunt she could pull. But you bring that to the table every time you randomly fuck somebody else. Now, [when] you young, you gonna do what you gonna do, but after a while, it gets old. Like, you get tired; it's too many different personalities to deal with. It's too much some-times. It ain't even worth it 'cause at the end of the day, you end up losing.

Dave wants and aspires to be in a committed relationship. While outsiders may think that he has plenty of choices, given the ratio of employed black men to black women, Dave believes that this assumption is problematic: his situation as a dealer is not ideal and quality partners regardless of gender are hard to fine.

After years of getting to know Dave, I was finally able to conduct and record formal interviews. Many took place in my car outside coffee shops and stores of his choosing, usually after he got off of work. I opted to inter-view him in my car because I was aware that he always carried a gun and a small amount of drugs. This safety precaution (in case someone ever tried to rob him) on my part soon became our routine. Dave was fascinated that I listened to talk radio, particularly NPR, which was always playing on the radio when he arrived. Since many of our discussions took place in the early evening, the NPR program *Marketplace* was usually on the radio. Dave, who was skeptical that anyone would consistently listen to public radio, once quizzed me about the show. While I was constantly observing and question-ing him, Dave reversed the gaze and eventually used my interest in econom-ics to make a larger point about his dating choices.

A month later, after Dave had broken up with his girlfriend of eight years and was already with another woman, I inquired how he could be in a new committed relationship so quickly. Dave replied, "Haven't you been listen-ing to *Marketplace*? Pussy is at an all-time low." He explained that although he was a drug dealer with a loyal clientele, he had a job with benefits and was a good man. Plenty of women were looking for a man like him.

> It's like men got more choices than females, you know? It's like you get a girl, she got a college degree, and she's all that. But socially, she messed up 'cause she don't know how to treat a man or know what a man's supposed to do. Like, if he go out, you'll call him and stalk him every five, ten minutes 'cause you so scared that somebody gonna take him from you. You know what I'm saying? But you not secure in your womanhood. But that comes from making bad decisions. Like, you constantly make a bad decision fucking all these terrible niggas. You know what I'm saying? I mean, there's good women out there. A lot of girls have been through shit, and those are the type that, at the end of the day when they get a little older, they realize, they settle down, and then they find a man. "He trying to get shit together and whatever." They work with you. If you ever notice, older females only mess with guys they call "fixer-uppers" or whatever. 'Cause it's like she see through the bullshit 'cause she done been through enough of it. She thirty-five, forty. She done went through all the ballers that sell drugs and all that shit. She know that shit ain't gonna last for so long, and she realize she want [to] work with the working man. You know what I'm saying? Slow and steady, you know what I'm saying? The fast grind, you burn out fast. Slow and steady win the race, man.

While I found it funny that he had turned my practice of listening to NPR into an opportunity to make a point about his chances in the relationship market, I instantly thought of the assertion that Wilson (1987) made in *The Truly Disadvantaged* with regard to the marriageable pool. Dave, like most of the men I met on Lyford Street, was never single. Despite their liabilities, working men were highly sought after by the women in their community.

Dave's understanding of the dating pool was situated in the reality of the heterosexual scene in Bristol Hill. Given the dynamics of the drug trade, women who involve themselves with dealers, particularly young ones, will eventually face the fact that their partners' exploits end badly. While his account was not explicit, he said that women, like their male counterparts in poverty, understand the economic challenges facing African American men and, with that understanding, are willing to date men whom they may have overlooked in the past.

Men like Dave have choices, but given the set of available potential partners, these men are still vulnerable for a host of reasons, most of them economic. While Dave was attractive to women whose educational and occupational achievements he couldn't match, he was still vulnerable because of his illegal activity. With any potential partner, there was always the possibility that *his* problems could become *her* problems. Living with someone who is involved in drug dealing puts everyone at risk for arrest and other punishments. Moreover, if a woman uses his illegal activities against him because she is angry at him for other reasons, he can suffer serious consequences.

Fred

I met Fred, who was then fifty-two years old, when I started volunteering in Bristol Hill. He was one of the first people willing to speak to me about changes in the community and his experiences on Lyford Street when I began scouting the neighborhood for volunteers for this study. As he became a major source of information, he introduced me to his family and friends in the neighborhood, including Dave. Fred had been living for six years with his niece, from whom he rented a room for $300 a month. We began to meet regularly, often after he finished work. I later found out that he had initially wanted me to date his niece, but even after I told him that I was in a relationship, we remained friends.

He earned, on average, $400 a week and maintained two regular sources of employment, one at a cleaning company and another at a seasonal construction job he had held for nine years. I often met with him during his temporary third job in a suburban area outside of Bristol Hill, where he worked as a valet and was paid only in tips. Most of the jobs Fred worked paid him under the table, which he preferred because it enabled him to avoid creditors trying to garnish his wages. Although Fred was constantly working, his goal of economic independence remained elusive at best. He paid child support only sporadically and had unpaid student loans, traffic fines, and back income taxes.

Fred married and joined the navy when he was eighteen because his girlfriend was pregnant; when I met him, he and his wife had been separated for fourteen years. They had two sons. The elder, aged thirty-three, was permanently disabled after a car accident left him with a spinal cord injury that compromised his ability to walk. For some time, Fred had visited his son regularly and done physical therapy with him. His much younger son, aged seventeen, had been battling leukemia since the age of six and continued to live with his mother. He was hospitalized for several weeks during the time I interviewed Fred.

Fred's wife worked as an administrator in city government, and they maintained what he described as a cordial relationship. Although she sued him for child support after they separated, they mutually decided not to divorce. Their marriage ended partly because of his long history of drug addiction, as well as the stress generated by their sons' disability and illness. He visited her home regularly, mostly to see his younger son. Although they were no longer together, she was instrumental in helping him buy a car and get car insurance, which she continued to pay for despite their separation.

His wife was in a romantic relationship, but Fred believed she was just dating. Fred had been consistently involved with two women since I met him. I once joked with him that he was incapable of being single while at the same time being incapable of maintaining a relationship. He quickly pointed out that his two sexual relationships started as casual dating and were long term, going back several years. In the past he had lived with each of the women, and he continued to spend several days with each of them during different parts of the month. He even had tattoos of both women's names, one on his arm and the other on his shoulder.

Fred described how these relationships developed into an understanding based on what he and his partners could realistically achieve. In his involvement with these two women, he was very much aware that he could not place any demands on them concerning their personal lives, nor could they place any such demands on him. Each relationship was a failed monogamous relationship. These women were part of a network of lovers and friends who built a trusting and reciprocal, although limited, relationship based on the likelihood that Fred would do what was asked of him. These networks benefited both Fred and the women with whom he was involved and created some stability and normality in all of their lives. The dynamics of these associations grew out of both parties being unable to satisfy the demands of a traditional relationship. After these relationships ceased to be monogamous, they became and remained more fluid; the requirements were less stringent with regard to commitment and time.

One of Fred's partners worked as a bus driver. She was three years older than he and had three adult children, two daughters and a son. Her son, who was in his early twenties, his girlfriend, and their two-year-old child resided with her in a house that she owned. Fred complained that he felt uncomfortable living in "her" house, where he was not able to dictate who came and who went. The only serious complaint I heard from him was that he did not have a home of his own.

His other partner, who was in her mid-forties, lived in housing project and worked as a hairstylist and beautician. Fred had been involved with her off and on for at least eight years. She had two adult daughters, and a sixteen-year-old son who resided with her. Fred had dated her exclusively for more than a year, but she ended the relationship after a man she was seeing before him was released from prison. Fred maintained that his relationship with her was purely sexual, but he often complained about her inability to commit to him. He showed me text exchanges where she clearly stated that she had no desire to be in a relationship with him but appreciated the time they spent together.

Although each relationship transitioned to a sexual attachment after the failure of a committed partnership, their associations remained meaningful and long term. He spent birthdays with the women, took them to casinos for long weekends, provided transportation, performed odd jobs, and mentored their children. He admitted that he sincerely loved both women, but I found he had a tendency to overstress the sexual nature of these relationships. It became clear to me after meeting both of his partners that these relationships were much more than sexual; they had developed into a type of alternative long-term intimate friendship that came with a certain level of autonomy, limiting the demands placed on all involved. Although the sex was important, the companionship, the free room and board, the small loans they extended to him, and his reciprocal assistance with their household and family needs highlighted how these women represented stable, dependable networks for both Fred and his partners.

I was initially unaware of Fred's extensive history of drug use. He had the appearance of good health; at five feet eleven and 190 pounds, he was relatively muscular, worked out at least three times a week, and maintained a healthy diet. When I complimented him on his youthful exterior, Fred used his shirt to wipe the makeup from under his eyes, revealing the deep purple-black wrinkles and dark circles that were the result of his history of heavy drug use, including more than ten years of heroin use and seven years of crack addiction. His preferred drug of choice was marijuana, which he said calmed him down and allowed him to sleep.

Fred avoided discussing his drug use; it was only after I told him about several of my relatives who battled addiction that he opened up about his own history. While he cited his addiction issues as the cause of his ruined marriage, he made it clear that he had no desire to quit smoking marijuana. Given his past, his ability to stay off of hard drugs such as crack and heroin was remarkable. When I asked whether he had ever attended rehab or spent time in recovery, he said no.

In many ways, Fred embodied the history of the drug trade in Bristol Hill over the past thirty-five years. His history with substance abuse followed a path from heroin to crack cocaine, back to heroin, then to powder cocaine, and, finally, to marijuana (Jacobs 1999). Fred, who had never been arrested or unemployed while I was in the field, prided himself on currently being clean from heroin and crack cocaine. While he continued to smoke marijuana and occasionally used cocaine, Fred was a functional addict. He attributed his success in transitioning down to lesser drugs to their effects on him and those around him and the stigma associated with crack and heroin addiction.

Fred, like many African American men, has held a marginal position in the labor market, earned lower wages, and therefore been less able to achieve his masculine ideals. While he cannot control his job prospects and lacks the means to live alone, he highlighted the one thing that he was able to provide: sex.

In his classic study *Tally's Corner* (1967), Elliott Liebow developed a "theory of manly flaws," describing marriage failures that are a result of the man's "personal inability or unwillingness to adjust to the built-in demands of the marriage relationship." Liebow made it very clear that racial discrimination made it impossible for black men to fulfill the ideal of the male breadwinner, which the women they knew espoused. Here I seek to understand how men account for the failures and successes of their intimate partner relationships. Fred's descriptions appeared to emphasize his sexual prowess. It seemed clear to me that he did so because it was the one aspect of his life he felt he had control over and that fit into a recognized form of masculinity (Duck 2009).

Fred used sex as a way of both affirming his masculinity and maintaining an intimate bond. The intimacy associated with these relationships allowed Fred to make demands that did not violate his desire for self-sufficiency. He framed these relationships sexually as way to cover up his inability to satisfy his partners' economic and emotional needs. Emphasizing the sexual nature of these relationships offered him a network of intimate partners who accepted him on his own terms. These relationships were defined not by what he could not do but by what he could achieve given his circumstances.

Marcus

I met Marcus after I found his wallet in the snow. Instantly, I thought it would be easier for me to give him his wallet rather than calling the police or dropping it in a mailbox. The open parking spot uncovered by snow gave me the impression that he had lost it relatively recently. In the wallet I discovered a driver's license from another state and more than four business cards belonging to attorneys. The wallet also contained his car insurance identification card. I tried searching for Marcus online but came up empty, so I called his insurance company who agreed to give him my phone number.

When Marcus called me, I asked him to meet me at a diner in a town five minutes outside of Bristol Hill. Marcus, who was twenty-three at the time, arrived in a gray 1987 Honda Accord. I gave him his wallet, and as he went through it he offered to give me the thirty dollars in cash it contained, but I refused to take the money. He thanked me profusely and said, "If you ever need anything, let me know." I revealed to him that I was working on a book about Bristol Hill and the Lyford Street neighborhood and asked him whether he lived there. He said he did not, but his aunt did, and he was visiting her for the holiday. He said he had often spent time in the neighborhood while he was growing up, so I asked whether he would be interested in doing an interview. He agreed.

Marcus told me that he used to be a bartender and worked primarily for tips but was currently employed as a telemarketer. He had pursued a degree in communications but never finished and still had student loan debt. Knowing all this relaxed me a bit, and I confessed that I had been somewhat worried because he had so many cards for attorneys in his wallet. He explained that the cards were a few months old and stemmed from a disputed child-support case with the mother of his son.

He had lived with her prior to his son's birth, but a year later they separated. The state had used a standard formula to calculate his child-support payments, and under the law nearly one-third of his take-home pay was garnished. Two years after the birth of his son, his former girlfriend returned to college and began working, moving off of welfare, yet she kept the state-mandated child-support payments in place. When she finished college, Marcus renegotiated the child-support arrangement directly with her. The situation had been at times problematic because, according to Marcus, whenever they had a dispute, she threatened to go back to the old arrangement of state-mandated payments that would be deducted from his paychecks.

Marcus was determined to maintain a relationship with his now six-year-old son, in part because his mother instilled in him the value of good parenting.

My mother raised me. We're three boys. OK, she took good care of us. And a man was never present in the household, but she always found a way to connect us with positive men in neighborhood that would really help her out. So when it was my opportunity to have kids, I knew that the men figure, that was missing in my life, and I didn't want that to happen to my children. But I'm one of the fortunate ones that didn't go to the bad side, 'cause I had a very strong-willed mother. So I know that I didn't want my kids to go through the same feelings that I went through. Football games . . . there's a woman there;

your father not there. So it was always that I love my mother dearly, and she was the greatest woman, but I'm sorry, you cannot be a mother and a father. So she was a great mother, and she found other people to take the men figure.

He described his relationship with his own father as "nonexistent": "I didn't have a father. I never did. I just recently met my father three years ago." When I asked how they met, he replied that he had found him through his father's other children on a social media website. "Well, actually, I met my younger sister first. I figured . . . Well, I do have two younger sisters. Of course, they had to be on Facebook, or . . . I knew her name. I put it in Myspace, found my sister. Sent her a message, asked if I looked familiar. You know, I explained to her who I was. That's how it started. I initiated with my younger sister. Me and my younger sister hit it off real well. And it was just uphill from there."

About a year later, he talked with his father on the phone for the first time. When I asked how that felt, Marcus responded:

I thought I would be angry. I thought I would probably want to fight him, but what actually killed all of that was the fact that my father apologized. . . . He just said, "You know, I can't really change anything that I've been in the past, but I am really sorry for not being there for you." You know, you could tell that the man was genuine. He wasn't full of it. To me, it just took everything away because I guess me being a man. . . . I'm not a child, an emotional teenager, anything like that. In fact, that's all I really needed, as far as from him at that point in time. Of course, I missed out on a lot of things. He's missed out on a lot of things that could've still made me different. But at the end of the day, all the man can do is apologize and show me something different now. If you dwell in the past, you have a thousand roads with no future. I'm over it.

Marcus's motivations for being present in his son's life are many, but his life choices are quite different from his father's. His mother's role as a determined, supportive parent, the other adult men who were present in his life, his ability to forgive his father, and his struggle to play a constructive role in his son's life have all shaped his assumption of paternal responsibility. The contrast illustrates that each generation faces real challenges, but men who have grown up without a father do not have to repeat that pattern.

Marcus's case has implications for policy as well. Black men in this study via their narratives made important suggestions about changes that could enable them to fulfill their middle-class aspirations, if only policy makers would listen to their point of view. A number of scholars have examined states' tendency to use a cost-sharing model for child support rather than an income-sharing model, which would take a father's own need for solvency into account (Collins and Mayer 2010; Pate and Johnson 2000). Moreover, public policy should assume that poor women are having children by poor men. Even in the best case, average wages in Bristol Hill range from the legal minimum of $7.25 per hour to $9 per hour. Marcus's account demonstrates that we should pay attention to other types of debt the parents have when figuring child-support amounts; Marcus owed student loans for a degree he never finished. Marcus's debts and his inability to pay the legally mandated child support had previously kept him from taking a job where he was paid officially rather than under the table for tending bar. In this way, unfair child-support arrangements may negatively affect men's labor force participation. Finally, we can learn a lesson from how Marcus renegotiated his payments: a child's mother might be willing to accept the support that the father could reasonably afford, while still maintaining her right to return to the legal arrangements imposed by the state if their agreement failed.

Justin

Like many of the men in this study, Justin had been a childhood lookout and young dealer. His stint in the drug trade was limited to his high school years, and he was relatively successful in finding employment after graduation. Although he attended community college for two years, he never finished his degree in child psychology. While in high school, he experimented with alcohol and marijuana but never viewed himself as a person with a substance abuse problem. When he was nineteen, however, Justin was arrested for unpaid tickets and a DUI after he refused to take a Breathalyzer test, and he later pleaded guilty to the DUI. Because of his personal involvement with the penal system, Justin has many well-founded opinions about the culture of incarceration.

> There's so many black men in prison. It's common knowledge that because the prison system with, you know, private industry, you need consumers. Who's the best consumer? Black men. You know why? 'Cause the cop's whole job is to make quota, to show police activity. Can't have all these crimes without no activity. So the good part is they riding around, but the bad part is they mess with people and get petty. . . . It's petty crimes and stuff that ain't even existed, and you locking people up for it just to make quota, but you're not getting to the root of the problem, which is arresting the people that's really doing crime. Like, you'll lock somebody up for having a bag over a beer or

something, but you know so-and-so is a known criminal on the block, but you won't mess with him, 'cause you know he gonna shoot at you. You ain't gonna mess with [*laughs*] hard criminals; you just gonna nitpick and politic with the people you know really ain't doing so much, just so you can make your numbers. Now, if you a cop and you do what you supposed to do and you don't make your numbers, then they say something wrong. The whole thing is geared to put the black man in jail. It don't matter what you do.

Like most of the employed men in the neighborhood, Justin earned an hourly wage; he made nine dollars an hour as a security guard. His credit was poor, so he usually lived with roommates. Because he had moved at least three times in the previous two years, he never received a summons for his court appearance for the DUI, which led to a warrant being issued for his arrest. At twenty-six, Justin still owed more than $3,000 stemming from the seven-year-old criminal case.

Recently, Justin was unlawfully evicted from his home and arrested on the outstanding warrant for unpaid court fees and fines. He was originally given two weeks' notice to vacate the house he shared with a roommate, but when he was out with a friend the locks were changed with all of his possessions still inside. When he attempted to retrieve his belongings, he was arrested after the police officer ran a background check. He was released several days later.

Justin returned again to collect his property, which resulted in his being rearrested.

So I get out, I don't have anything, I don't have a phone, I don't have keys, I only had six dollars on me. . . . So that's the main thing I'm doing all day, trying to figure out how I can get my ID for work and some work clothes so I can at least keep my job because I had been off work for three or four days. Luckily, I was already off on Tuesdays, and Monday was a holiday, but I'm trying to get to work. I speak to the landlord, he tells me he's going to meet me. He doesn't show up until forty-five minutes later, and then he tells me, "No, I can't let you in to get your things." I am furious, so I decide to get my belongings. So basically I waited for him to leave. I go in there, come out, he's waiting outside; mind you, this is three hours later. He just so happens to be pulling up when I was leaving. Next thing I know, I hear police sirens. I'm confused. I'm arrested again, taken to jail, again. . . . First they were going to charge me with breaking and entering, but there was no proof of breaking or entering, so then they tried to charge me with burglary but couldn't because I was taking my own belongings, so they charged me with criminal trespassing.

It is possible that had Justin called the police when he was unlawfully evicted, he could have retrieved his belongings without so much hassle. Justin did not call the police because he felt that they would treat him as a criminal instead of seeing him as the victim in this situation. Given what transpired, we see that his general assumption with regard to law enforcement was correct. Landlords rent to tenants like Justin knowing that their legal situation puts them in a precarious position and potentially works against them. Unlike their tenants, landlords have a relatively free hand in operating outside the law.

Brent

I met a ninth-grader named Brent when I volunteered at a church-sponsored after-school program. Brent stood out because he not only participated in the program but also tutored younger participants. Counselors and tutors in the program recognized that he had great promise; he was a successful student and a talented writer. His parents kept him constantly busy.

Brent was especially memorable because he exposed me to a young-adult book series that highlighted the challenges of young urban youth. The Bluford Series is composed of twenty or so novels set at a fictional high school in Los Angeles named after Guion Stewart Bluford Jr., the first African American in space. After I told him I was from Detroit, Brent pointed out that one of his favorite characters from the series was from Detroit as well.

Four years after meeting him, I rediscovered Brent during his senior year of high school after he was charged with bringing a weapon to school. This incident prompted both a criminal hearing and a school disciplinary hearing. Just months before his expected graduation, the school district sought to expel him, not understanding that Brent was participating in a college preparatory program sponsored by a local religious organization. The Prestige Project was designed to mentor and monitor students' academic achievement from ninth grade through college. Fortunately, the director of the program worked diligently to organize teachers, politicians, counselors, and school administrators on his behalf.

Since I knew Brent from the after-school program, I followed the situation closely. I learned that the criminal and disciplinary charges were lodged when he brought a *shuriken* (throwing star) to school. Through the Prestige Project, Brent was taking classes in Japanese. He brought the *shuriken* to school as part of a homework assignment that required students to bring items from home that show Japanese cultural influence. The *shuriken* was found in his bag as he went through the school's metal detectors. Security at

Bristol Hill High was provided by city police officers, who worked under a policy of zero tolerance for weapons. So they arrested him. The Bristol Hill High School code of conduct policy listed a number of offenses that would result in a mandatory hearing, including violence and the possession of weapons and drugs; it did not define what might be considered a weapon.

Brent had no history of violence, yet he faced being expelled for this technical violation of school policy. Upon hearing all the details of Brent's case, the principal, several of his teachers, counselors from the Prestige Project, and other mentors agreed that the situation should have been handled differently and the decision about how to respond should have been made by the school principal rather than the police officers. Yet, according to the guidelines, anyone who worked in the school could enforce the zero-tolerance policy, which usually involved an expulsion hearing.

Brent first had to appear before the city court, which charged him with possession of a deadly weapon. After testimony from teachers, counselors, and people from the community, he was cleared. He still had to go before the school disciplinary court, which handled expulsions.

The director of the Prestige Program, Fatima Hagar, spoke to several of the hearing officers, who gave her a grim warning that he would most likely be expelled. They admonished her that weapons charges were serious offenses and that if they let Brent go, they would have to treat other cases similarly. To ensure Brent's chances for a successful graduation, she reached out to the superintendent, who made sure Brent's disciplinary hearing was scheduled after he received his diploma.

Victor Rios (2011) developed the concept of the "youth control complex," a ubiquitous system that functions to monitor, stigmatize, criminalize, and collectively punish young people of color. The youth control complex in this case relates to punishment in schools, where security is provided by local police and school officials and even those in positions of power have little discretion once a zero-tolerance policy is invoked. This case shows how the school-to-prison pipeline works and who has discretion to prevent this from happening. Zero-tolerance policies can be applied in different ways, particularly in regard to what is considered a weapon. If the police are in charge of enforcing the policy, the presence of any object that could conceivably be used as a weapon is taken seriously. This blurring of the lines between what is and what is not permitted makes it difficult for students and their parents to stay within the guidelines.

Ultimately, if the policy violation leads to an arrest and criminal charges lead to a criminal record, a student is propelled into the school-to-prison pipeline. Brent's case had a relatively positive outcome, mostly because he had numerous powerful advocates, but zero-tolerance policies that invoke sanctions without any discretion are dangerous. Once a charge is made, a damaging outcome is highly likely.

Navigating a System of Collective Punishment

The economic changes brought about by deindustrialization and the rise of the low-wage service sector have shaped the social situation of African American men living in Bristol Hill. But isolating the economy, the school system, the criminal justice system, or any other structural factor that disproportionately burdens the poor provides us with limited insight; it is the interplay among these institutions that inhibits men's life chances. It creates a system that reinforces collective punishment for a population that is already in dire straits (Rios 2011; Laub and Sampson 1995, 2001, 2003). If we recognize the all-encompassing effects of the combination of mass incarceration and criminal records, unemployment and underemployment, financially starved educational institutions, consumer and student debt, and violence on the experiences black men, we can make a more accurate diagnosis and begin to devise effective remedies.

In communities such as Bristol Hill, African American men and boys must navigate a terrain fraught with economic hardship, the constant threat of criminalization, and fragile social networks. They are bombarded with challenges that compound one another. To survive, they cannot work with but must get around and effectively subvert major institutions, especially law enforcement, the economy, and the educational system. Their situations require attention to urgent problems of work and family and necessitate that they forgo making long-term plans. Burdened with debt and criminal records, they are seldom able to realize whatever aspirations they do develop to transform their lives. They correctly perceive that they have precious few allies or resources in that effort. Indeed, in the social world of Lyford Street, major state institutions are at best severely compromised and at worst dysfunctional.

Those who are not already incarcerated on drug charges find themselves in a neo-debtors' prison. Indeed, their inability to pay the accumulated debts that arise from unemployment and low wages carries the real possibility of imprisonment. Practices such as zero-tolerance policies in the schools and the near-universal criminalization of young black men compromise their future prospects. In this context, we can begin to understand the choices made by men who grew up in Bristol Hill. Individuals who are raised and live in areas like Lyford Street confront a matrix of factors that stymie their ambition to get ahead.

These men make sense of their lives by incorporating the local order in their community, which is in direct conflict with the wider societal order. Their immediate loyalties are to their family and friends, and working within that framework requires men to make decisions about the matters that are the most pressing. Concentrated poverty (Wilson 1987) creates social conditions that form a coherent system in which many common situations create new problems that collectively carry severe penalties. Given the number of challenges these men face, concentrated poverty renders an already difficult situation utterly intractable. The constraints are multiple, overlapping, and to some extent mutually exacerbating: absence of higher-wage jobs, inadequate education, radical contraction of social safety nets, a judicial-police system whose attentions make things worse, child-support laws that work against people with limited resources and job prospects. Yet within these narratives, many of the men have found workable solutions to the problems they face that could easily be incorporated by policy makers.

SEVEN

Benita's Story: Coping with Poverty in the Age of Welfare Reform

Benita Williams, like many other poor, single, black women, struggled to make ends meet in a game where the odds seemed to be stacked against her. She first became pregnant at the age of fourteen. She had another child with the same man a year later, and two more children with a different man when she was seventeen and eighteen. When I met her, she and her four children were living in a very small three-bedroom brick row house. Although they were better housed than many poor families, their tenancy involved constant deception and was only temporary. Benita's story reveals the strategies that she and many in similar positions use to deal with their lack of resources and the instability of their support networks (Newman 2000). In this chapter, I present narrative accounts of the practices she used to navigate poverty, which required great personal resiliency. I also detail the dynamics of her various networks, examining how she maintains them and what forces have combined to make them increasingly precarious.

Adopting an interaction-order approach to the Lyford Street community illuminates the extent to which living in poverty requires people to improvise strategies to meet each new difficulty at it arises. We can begin to understand how people become impoverished and remain stalled in that condition. Benita's story is an illustration of what happens in poor neighborhoods where double binds are prevalent, and through it we can explore societal policies aimed at addressing and remedying poverty.

Meeting Benita's Children

I encountered Benita's children on my first day as a volunteer at a day camp during the summer of 2006, when her son Ali chose me to play checkers with him. Initially, I indulged him by playing along while watching him make illegal moves and allowing him to beat me four games straight. He wasn't the only one to cheat; I lost many rigged card games to other kids. They even cheated at kickball and basketball, but I went along, curious to see how far it would go. Not only did I want to be treated like an outsider who needed to learn the rules, but also I wanted to know whom I could trust with regard to information and fair play. The next day I decided to play by their adjustments to the rules; I made moves and played cards illegally. They quickly corrected me: "No, nu-uh, you can't do that." "But *you* did it," I said. "I know, because you didn't know the games." When I began to cheat and then confronted them with their own cheating as they called me out, the cheating ended within a day.

Later that summer, I played Monopoly with Ali and three other black boys who lived in the Lyford Street neighborhood. During the game, the four boys between the ages of seven and ten unintentionally provided me with telling glimpses of what their lives were like outside of the day camp. Their knowledge of the rules of the game was more than adequate; they had a basic understanding of the process of rolling the dice and making their moves. Their eagerness to keep the game going at a fast pace was apparent as they hurried each other along to take their turns. Their focus on the need to collect money and pay rent seemed to have a special meaning in the context of their own lives and contributed to the high level of speed and intensity. They eagerly encouraged one another to buy property, make as much money as possible, and show their accumulation of wealth. When there was a disagreement over payments due or possible anticipation of landing on another player's property, the loud talking and overlapping conversation that ensued alluded to their own personal experiences.

Given the themes of property, rent, utilities, money, debt, and jail that pervade the game, the play elicited many comments from the children that seemed to be based on real-life situations familiar to them. They demanded, "Pay me my money," and asked, "Oh, ho, where's my rent?" "Pay your lights and water bill or I'm going to turn them off," they threatened. As a last resort, they ordered, "Get off my property." Competition could quickly turn to camaraderie, however, as they exhibited a strong willingness to help each other out of a bind; there were also egalitarian moments during the game. For example, when Victor went bankrupt, Ali said that he could join his team, with no objections from the other players. In another instance, the entire group conspired to prevent a fellow player from going to jail. Their artful manipulation of the rules afforded intriguing insights into their concerns. Everyone was given a chance to save face. This game of Monopoly, which is based on a premise of unfairness where winner takes all, gave me a glimpse into the world in which these kids lived.

My fascination with these children was focused on Ali, Benita's seven-year-old son. The three other boys who also played with us were eight-year-old Kamal, the second youngest of the four boys and a skilled basketball player who bore an uncanny resemblance to LeBron James; nine-year-old David, a dark-skinned infrequent participant at the day camp; and nine-year-old Victor, a short-haired, fair-skinned kid who was often mistaken for a Latino.

After going over the rules, I told the boys that whoever rolled the highest number could go first. Ali instantly said, "Come on, Big Seven," and Victor said, "Big Red," both references to craps. During an hour of play, I heard interesting accounts of evictions and utilities being shut off, as well as a shared desire to avoid going to jail. I learned over the course of the summer that Ali's father was in jail. Most striking during game play were the clear understandings these children had of the importance of money and the sanctions associated with poverty, of the impact of prison and the resistance to being incarcerated, of property ownership and eviction, and of the risk of utilities being shut off because of outstanding bills. Monopoly exposed a set of familiar concerns for these children while simultaneously revealing their resiliency.

Benita's Story

In the subsequent weeks, I met Benita, my name for the mother of Ali and one other boy who participated in the camp (her two other children did not attend). From her I learned about the daily realities these boys faced. It took me over a year to get to know Benita before I formally interviewed her. At that point she was twenty-six years old. She had dropped out of high school in the tenth grade and left home at seventeen to live with the father of her two oldest children; they lived together for five years. She later earned her GED at age twenty-four.

Her smile was stunning, and I found her extremely disarming. At five feet five, with a medium-brown complexion, high cheekbones, and thick black shoulder-length hair, Benita reminded me immediately of a young Janet Jackson. Her voice was low and soft but rose when she was excited or upset. She constantly smiled when we talked, and she had a tendency to take deep breaths when she tried to explain things to me. Yet, with her face at rest when she listened intently, she looked sad and melancholy. Her eyes seemed to water as if she were constantly on the verge of tears.

Benita had a wonderful sense of humor, and at times when I didn't get a joke, she would explain to me why her comments were funny. For example, when her six-year-old son Joaquin came home from his first day of first grade and asked her to buy him boxers instead of briefs, she laughed and looked at Joaquin and joked with him, saying, "Aw, my baby want to look sexy for those first-grade girls." Embarrassed, Joaquin threw his hand up and ran upstairs to his bedroom. I joked with her, stating that it was the first time that I had ever heard the words "sexy" and "first grade" in the same sentence. We laughed, but she explained that Joaquin wanted to start sagging his pants like the older boys, for whom boxers, not briefs, were the underwear of choice. I admired her sense of humor, which I soon recognized was a coping mechanism.

Benita and I talked weekly on the phone, and I would sometimes visit her at home and take her grocery shopping, to her nurse's aide job, or to pick up her kids from school. Our relationship was something of an equal exchange. I shared as much information about my life as she shared about hers. Our most intense conversation was about how the crack cocaine epidemic had changed cities all over the country. She told me:

> Crack was something else. I had family sold crack. My cousin use to sell crack in the late eighties. He was killed when I was in the second or third grade. To this day nobody knows who did it. They found his body in a vacant lot in another city, shot up. My mother and my aunt had a falling out because my cousin tried to get my brother to sell. Crack was crazy, man; I mean people were, like, leaving their babies at our house, coming back days later. Didn't make any sense. The robbing, the raids, family members stealing from you. . . . Crack was something else.

She raised similar concerns regarding her oldest children's father, who battled heroin addiction. While she expressed disappointment that he was unable to help her with child care and her finances, she preferred to limit his contact with their children because of his addiction. Benita explained that her children usually interacted with their father while the grandparents were present. While his family helped her sporadically, disagreements over the way she parented often created long periods with limited or no communication. On numerous occasions I tried to get Benita to discuss the father's limited involvement, but she refused. She blamed his addiction as the problem, not him, reminding me that "he still the father" of her children and that she was "not going to badmouth their dad."

The family resources available to Benita were tenuous. She understood the limitations of those around her but was equally concerned about the negative influences that certain people might have on her children and the judgments of others regarding her own parenting abilities. Her investment in these relationships appeared to depend on her freedom to parent as she saw fit. Benita reported losing some access to her female kin networks over time, but she was quick to point out that a crisis (such as a threat of imprisonment) or a celebration (such as her daughter graduating from high school) could alleviate strained relationships. While these networks were not permanently harmed, they could become compromised for long periods of time.

Local churches and religious organizations have been a constant and vitally important resource in communities such as Bristol Hill. The availability of space and the philosophy of unconditional opportunities for membership within such institutions have saved many families by providing numerous resources, such as after-school programs. Yet these community resources are often secondary to the elaborate and intertwined kin networks that form the fragile safety net that such families so desperately need when things go wrong. Families under extreme stress and facing great uncertainly heavily relied on their relatives, friends, and religious institutions for sustainability in their day-to-day lives.

Even when Benita had seemingly exhausted her options, these networks together created a buffer that often led to acts of goodwill from both relatives and strangers alike. For example, when Benita was arrested, both sets of her in-laws contributed to her bail, and a paternal aunt watched all four of her children for a few days upon her release; in addition, all of her siblings sent her money. After this crisis, her father came from another state to move in with her and help pay her rent and bills and care for her children. Benita had also lived with her mother during her first pregnancy; her father's insurance paid for costs associated with the birth.

But this kinship network could "tap out." Her brother, who lived out of state, refused to accept her calls after not hearing from her for four years. (Their estrangement appeared to be related to a violent incident that she declined to discuss in depth, simply stating that she refused to let any man put his hands on her.) Her sister, who also lived out of state, was cautious about contacting Benita because of her previous relationships with drug dealers and her constant relocations. In addition, Benita's father complained when she failed to repay a series of loans. Benita's mother, who lived the closest to her, avoided her because she didn't like being used for child care.

This limited contact was partially her choice as well. "My family is too judgmental, so I try to keep them out of my business," she said. Her children continued to visit her mother and her sister occasionally; Benita's mother even had primary custody of her two older children for a time, cementing a significant relationship with them. Benita pointed out that she was hesitant to ask her parents for help because they were both living on fixed incomes. Even though she received their help in the past, she now had only limited contact with them because, as she put it, her mother and sister viewed her as "too needy."

While Benita criticized her children's paternal relatives, their fathers' siblings and extended kin nonetheless offered various opportunities to her children, even while she and their fathers rarely communicated. In Benita's children's teenage years, they took a more active approach to their relationships with their fathers but also a more critical view of them, as they worked to establish and nurture relationships with cousins, aunts, uncles, and even former spouses of their fathers.

Although her children's fathers' kin might have served as an additional support system, their animosity toward Benita for getting pregnant and taking resources (profits from the drug trade) from his immediate family made them less willing to help. As with her own family, she was, at times, reluctant to engage with the children's paternal grandparents because she wanted to keep her life private. The parents of her two older children's father called on child protective services on multiple occasions to have her children removed from her home. The charges ranged from abandonment to poor living conditions, and in the end each case was closed with no findings of abuse or neglect. While these grandparents said that they did not want custody, Benita complained that they seized every opportunity to have her children taken away. Her two youngest children's paternal relatives will only see them when their father is present.

As I came to know Benita better, I realized that her access to familial assistance varied with the severity of the crisis and, importantly, how it might affect her children. While the long-term child care and loans that she had received in the past were now unavailable, her family's concern for the well-being of the children and their desire to come together for special events such as birthdays and holiday celebrations was still very apparent.

The kinship network on which so many poor black women rely has been severely compromised in Benita's case, and she has few places to turn to for support. Violence, addiction, and state involvement have limited her contact with kin. Her own frequent moves, previous intimate relationships, consistent debt, and child care needs have also compromised familial relationships. This analysis of the material and interpersonal resources on which black mothers living in poverty rely is inspired by Carol Stack's *All Our Kin* (1974), which described the networks that mothers formed within their neighborhoods based mostly on their own relatives and, depending on the circumstances, the families of their children's fathers. Benita's story shows not only the devastating consequences of recent changes in welfare policy on poor families' financial situation but also their corrosive effects of deepening impoverishment on their interpersonal support networks.

Work, Debt, and Fear of Arrest

The cycle of disruptions in Benita's life was relatively predictable. Every few months, she was evicted for not paying rent and had to move, she lost her job because of some crisis related to her children at home, or she changed her phone number because she couldn't pay the bill. We routinely lost touch and then reconnected. To keep herself motivated during turbulent times, Benita created an imaginary alter ego to help get through each day. She often reminded me that if she didn't stay positive and upbeat, she would be constantly depressed; her alter ego saw her life and world as perfect, and that's how she coped day by day. She said:

> My alter ego is perfect: she has her life together, and she has a beautiful career. She's living life. All the problems I'm going through, she is the total opposite. Everything is perfect with her. Literally when I am stressed and depressed, I revert to that in my head. I go to that space—that's what keeps me sane; that other person keeps me going. She's my strength. Seriously, she exists to me. Me being depressed and down—that's who I am.

This imaginary person had none of Benita's problems, such as insufficient child care, low wages, housing trouble, and men who were incapable of helping her because of their addiction and incarceration. Benita saw herself as having the potential to be anything she wanted to be but lacking the economic resources to move forward. She believed she was a "beautiful, caring, and compassionate person" and desperately wanted to figure out another, better path for herself and her children, but she just had too many obstacles to overcome.

Benita did work for a health-care company that provided assistance to seniors. Soon after I met her, Benita's unemployment and her pending application for welfare required her to participate in Work-First, a welfare-to-work program that a private agency contracted with the state to provide.

Applicants received training and assistance with job searches. Men were typically placed in automotive repair and carpentry programs, while women were steered toward child care or health care. Given Benita's level of experience, she consistently found employment in the range of nine dollars per hour. She said that most of the decent jobs paying ten dollars per hour were outside the city, while the few that were available in the city paid a little more than seven dollars an hour. Working conditions in the suburbs were also better than those in the city.

An Arrest for Unpaid Debts

In 2010 Benita was arrested for unpaid driving tickets. While most Americans rarely accumulate enough traffic tickets and unpaid fines to be arrested, this is surprisingly common in Bristol Hill. Debt from state-enforced sanctions was a common theme in many of my interviews and observations. In an attempt to curb the drug trade, local law enforcement agencies received additional state and federal funding to patrol the area. Traffic stops were a by-product of the extra vigilance, leading to disproportionate contact with law enforcement in poor communities. Law enforcement tended to police the places where poor neighborhoods transition into middle-class ones. Many jobs in the surrounding areas required low-wage workers; in order to access those jobs, workers had to cross those boundaries. Although Benita was not a direct target of increased police surveillance, she was caught in the net.

Public transportation was available within Bristol Hill, but Benita usually worked in suburban areas accessible only by car. While driving to and from work, Benita received tickets for speeding, driving an uninsured vehicle, failing to wear her seat belt, and improperly displaying her license plate. She explained:

> I had the license plate in my window instead of on the back of the car. I can't remember why. I just got the plates to put on the car, and I didn't have the screws to screw it in, so I just stuck the plate in the window. And they pulled me over for that [*laughs*]. The city doesn't care about that. So it's like, it's outside the city—suburban areas, mainly, like, when I'm goin' to work, or, you know, goin' to look for a job—where you get a ticket.

She could not pay the tickets immediately, and penalties for unpaid fines increased the amount she owed to $2,200. After Benita was arrested for failing to pay the tickets, she served three days in jail and lost her driver's license.

A day after her arrest, I asked her how she got to work. "Yeah, I drove," she replied, "because there's . . . how am I gonna get there? I can't lose my job, so now I'm cautious. I have to watch for the police, and when I see them, I turn off and go a whole 'nother route and then get back on track, and then I'm off."

The Accident

While Benita was a very cautions driver, no amount of caution could have prevented what happened one morning on her way home from her night shift, when a young white man on his bike—on his way to work, but running late—rushed from the sidewalk into the street in front Benita's car. As she passed through the intersection, her car hit the front wheel of his bike; the impact threw the man off his bike onto her windshield. She instantly stopped to help him. Even though Benita was operating her car without a license or insurance and at that time owed more than $600 in fines, she called 911, and an ambulance and the police were dispatched. Meanwhile, she stayed at the scene.

Benita told me that this was her first car accident. When I spoke to her a few days afterward, she was still distressed. At the time of impact, the bicyclist's body cracked her windshield. Her initial fear was that she might have killed or paralyzed the man. Even though he was fully conscious and appeared to be fine, she relied on her medical knowledge and worried that the bicyclist might have had internal injuries, and she insisted that he wait until he was checked out by ambulance workers. She described being so distraught herself that the bicyclist hugged and comforted her while they waited.

When the police arrived on the scene, she recognized both officers from numerous previous traffic stops. She quickly explained that she did not have a license and that she was in the process of paying off the previous fines but stressed that she had to drive to work every day in order to support her family. Still in her nursing scrubs and obviously upset, she was then comforted and hugged by one of the officers, who explained that most people in her circumstances would have left the scene of the accident. Moreover, because she remained until they got there, the officer told her that he would not give her a citation or place her under arrest. No one was severely injured, and the bicyclist took responsibility for the accident. After the officers left, one of Benita's coworkers picked her up and they drove the bicyclist to work.

But Benita continued to ruminate on the accident and wonder why she hadn't been arrested. In discussing the incident, several of Benita's friends also speculated about why she hadn't been arrested and considered what role race may have played. Normally, hitting a white suburbanite could well have landed her in jail, particularly given her driving record and suspended license. Had the bicyclist been a poor person from Bristol Hill, they suggested, the victim probably would have attempted to exploit the circumstances for financial gain by filing a personal injury lawsuit. I, too, wondered why this encounter with the police did not end with a sanction. Moreover, I was perplexed about why Benita had stayed at the scene after realizing that the bicyclist was unhurt. Finally, given the number of mundane traffic stops and citations of the past, it became clear that police officers exercise a wide range of discretion with regard to not only car accidents but also traffic stops.

I believe that in the eyes of the police officers, Benita exceeded the ordinary expectations of the situation—that someone in her circumstances would have fled the scene of the accident. Erving Goffman (1983) argued that social anticipations are transformed into normative expectations, especially toward stigmatized groups. If the officers expected that the driver would leave the scene, then her remaining was abnormal and unexpected. In addition, she was so upset and remorseful that the police responded by comforting her. Had she not shown emotion, she could have received sanctions, but it would have been difficult for the officers to do that when she was clearly so remorseful. The role of the biker was also crucial, in that he comforted her and admitted wrongdoing. The situation appeared to have been resolved to the satisfaction of everyone involved, but in the end, Benita was very likely given a break.

"Kids Don't Make Adult Choices about Sex"

Three years before, Benita's eldest daughter missed a few days of school. Rumors quickly spread that the twelve-year-old was pregnant and that Benita, who was twenty-seven at the time, was going to be a grandmother. The story proved untrue, but it provided the occasion for a candid discussion with me about Benita's own pregnancies and how she tried to prevent her children, especially her daughters, from engaging in sex during their teen years. She was particularly concerned about such behavior because her work schedule forced her to leave her children unattended. Benita made a compelling argument for teaching adolescents, particularly girls, about what she defined as adult choices with lifelong consequences.

Given Benita's precarious situation with regard to wages, employment, and raising a family, I soon realized that a potential crisis was never far off. Each crisis not only required immediate attention but also exacerbated her impoverished situation. When I began following Benita's story, her daughter became sexually active and the paternal grandmother made a report to Child Youth Services (CYS), a government agency that investigates child abuse and neglect. When I was volunteering, I heard that the twelve-year-old girl had missed school because she was attacked by her mother for getting pregnant. Given the description of the mother and child involved, I suspected that the person in question was Benita. This rumor also turned out to be false, and when I contacted Benita about the stories being told around the neighborhood, she explained why she was being investigated:

> I slapped her! It was the second time that she was caught in the process of . . . about to engage in sex. The first time she was caught was a few months ago at a sleepover—with her friend's brother. We talked about it; she said she wasn't ready, but she was curious. I suggested birth control; she said she wasn't interested in boys. I discussed condoms, explaining that if she has the urge, she should protect herself. So, I thought we were good. We move over here [Lyford Street], and the kids are hanging out at a neighborhood party [organized by a local church]. I was suspicious because I already see that the boys outnumbered the girls, but I didn't think anything of it. Next thing I know, my youngest son comes running in the house and said that Kayla's in the backyard with a boy and his pants are down. She comes into the house all nonchalantly, so I asked her what was happening and she got smart: "I didn't know he was going to just whip it out." When I asked her why did she stay or why didn't she send the boy home, she got smart again: "Well, it not like I can have company in the house." She bumped me as she tried to rush past me, and I slapped her. She called her grandmother, who picked her up for a few days. The next thing I know, I'm being investigated for child abuse.

While Benita was not charged with child abuse, this incident exposed several features of her everyday life and networks, as well as past events in her life that shaped her actions. She pointed out that her parents never discussed sex or how to prevent an unwanted pregnancy and said that her early pregnancies could have been avoided had her parents, particularly her mother, explained the consequences of intercourse. Accordingly, Benita was very forthcoming about sex and sexuality with her two daughters, who were twelve and seven at the time of this incident. She diligently tried to monitor her daughters' sexuality, since she was constantly reminded of the stigma associated with teen mothers. As her daughters grew older, Benita went to great lengths to police their sexuality. In an effort to provide her daughters with the support Benita felt she herself lacked, she supplied tampons, made sure that they were having regular periods (all of the females in the house menstruated at the same time), had very detailed discussions about condom use, threatened eviction if a daughter became pregnant and did not opt for abortion, and even monitored their Facebook and text messages for sexual content.

When I spoke to Benita about her own pregnancies and her history of sexual activity, she said that her parents' strong Christian convictions made sex a taboo subject. She was even afraid to ask her older sister about sex because it might imply guilt. The topic was never discussed, either before or after she became sexually active. She blamed her mother for allowing her to have children so young and was very critical of her mother's failure to discuss sex openly. Benita was convinced that if her mother, who worked full-time, had spent more time with her, Benita's life would have been different: "My mother failed me, and I am still bitter about it. Because she is a woman, with two daughters, she should have stopped me; she should have said, 'No, I am not going to let you mess your life up.'"

When I asked her about her father's role, she said, "What about it? He tried to be a good dad—but as a woman, especially with two daughters, you have to say no!" She also felt that her father failed her because he was not around while she was growing up. Now her father was trying to make up for missing most of her childhood; he called often, made several visits to see his grandchildren, and even volunteered to move in with her to help pay her bills and raise the children. Benita said, however, that in the end her mother's failure was more serious because a daughter's bond with her mother is more important than that with her father.

Benita first became sexually active at age fourteen. A boy she liked passed her a note in class that read, "Do you like me? Circle yes or no." They had a shared understanding, she explained:

> Of course, you kiss and hug, show affection, but we thought if you're in a relationship, then you have sex, and that's exactly what we did. We were alone on his back porch and decided right then and there. A week later, we broke up. It was not like most people described as a special time. . . . You then realize you gave him your virginity, which is not something you can just get back; it is then gone for good.

Benita's second boyfriend was her first child's father, Curtis, an eighteen-year-old college student. They met when Benita, still just fourteen, was waiting outside school; he drove by and asked her for her phone number. They later talked on the phone and, according to Benita, instantly became "boyfriend and girlfriend." In retrospect, she said she thought that giving Curtis her number was one of the worst decisions that she ever made. She started skipping school to hang out with him because he was older and attractive. Curtis was using drugs and associated with an older group. One of his friends owned a bar, and Benita and Curtis often spent time there during the day because Curtis still lived with his parents. Her daughter was conceived in the bar from Benita's second sexual experience. She says she did not understand the meaning of sex until she was twenty-one. When I asked her to elaborate, she stated that by then she had a better understanding of what made her happy.

When Benita discovered she was pregnant the first time, she went to an abortion clinic with her mother and her older sister. She said the procedure cost about $150, depending on the duration of the pregnancy and whether the woman wanted to be sedated. When the staff explained the procedure to her, she became too scared and decided to have the baby and raise the child herself. Twelve years later, however, she had an abortion after ending her relationship with the father of her two younger children. She stated that with her first child, she romanticized the process of having a child and that, in retrospect, it was impossible for her to make a decision that took her future into consideration. While she made it clear that she did not regret having children, raising a family allowed her to empathize with what her mother and sister were trying to do by taking her to the abortion clinic.

The Housing Merry-Go-Round

Keeping her family housed was a constant struggle for Benita. When she was unemployed, her income was only $700 per month, woefully insufficient to cover the family's necessary expenses. She had been evicted at least four times while I was conducting this study. Although she had applied for public housing, an apartment might take up to three years to become available: the housing authority's shift to placing poor tenants in mixed-income housing had limited the number of available units. According to Benita, it was virtually impossible to get into public housing: the children of families who already resided there were moved to the top of the waiting list when they turned eighteen, pushing outsiders further down the list. A housing authority representative I interviewed later confirmed Benita's account.

Benita's tax refund had enabled her to get an apartment, since the deposit was always the biggest hurdle. However, she had to lie on the application about her employment status. She explained: "The landlord is just looking at all this money I got. He's not gonna check anything, you know, so I told him I had a job. I put it down on paper that I was working, and he got me the house." The problem was that her expenses exceeded her monthly income:

> I know I'll only get $700 a month, and that's gonna go towards the rent, so as far as the utilities. . . . That's how I ended up having to move, because I couldn't pay for the utilities. They ended up getting shut off, and then I can't live there without the utilities, so I have to take the $700 and try to find somewhere else to go. So they're not gettin' their rent. . . . So now I have to look for another house and take this $700 and wait for the next month for the other $700 to even have a first month's rent and security deposit to put on another house. So during that time I'm staying there [in the former apartment], and I know I can stay there for at least two months before they can evict me, with no utilities, so that's how it goes.

In the best of circumstances, she could remain in an apartment for a month or two before eviction proceedings would start and then for two more months after that. If she did not go to court, the bailiffs would remove her belongings from the house. If she pleaded hardship and asked for more time, the court could opt to give her up to thirty days to move out or come up with the money. After the court-ordered extension had passed, Benita would move out, concluding the eviction process (Desmond 2012a, 2012b). And so the merry-go-round continued to turn for her family—when she was lucky.

It was clear from her account of her finances that Benita could not afford housing. Although the average subsidized house in Bristol Hill rented for $500, unsubsidized rental units, especially for tenants with questionable credit, could range from $700 to $800 per month. Benita planned to float from house to house in four- to five-month cycles of eviction until a slot opened up in public housing. Her ongoing cycle of eviction and moving was typical; in this community, a large pool of people found it impossible to maintain housing payments without any outside assistance. In some sense, landlords must be satisfied with the occasional rent payments they can get through this process. Benita saw her own intention to break her contract as fair play, though, because slumlords were breaking the law, the houses were unlivable, or the landlord failed to pay utilities even when they were listed as included in the rent.

Limitations of Mutual Aid

When a financial emergency occurred—such as being arrested—Benita tried every possible avenue to secure funds, from seeking out bail bondsmen and pawning jewelry and electronics to using rent and utility money and even borrowing from strangers whom, she admitted, she was not likely to repay. She regularly used a payday loan service, which she contended was designed to put her deeper into debt. For example, for a $300 loan, she had to provide a bank statement and pay a $50 "interest" fee up front. The loan company called her employers for employment verification and a reference, and then she had to give the company a check for the amount of the loan. If she did not repay it by the next payday or pay the interest, they would deposit the check. If the check bounced, the company would attempt to deposit it every week. In one recent instance, the payday loan company tried to deposit her check five times, charging a $37 returned check fee each time. She could not repay the loan because she had borrowed money to get her car fixed and was unable to get to work until the car was running again. The fees ultimately totaled $235 on a $300 loan.

During the time of this study, Benita had a different phone number every time she contacted me or I tried to call her. She used a month-to-month service that allowed her to sign up for a phone and new number under any name and without a contract. The service was cheap, and the company did not keep track of late payments. For the last year and a half of this study, however, Benita had managed to keep the same phone number, which suggested more stability in her situation. Her credit score was up to 530, which was also an improvement. She still could not get credit through conventional means, so she had to resort to very high-cost loans when she needed them.

Both Benita's housing and employment histories followed a similar pattern. Within two years, she moved five times and had four different jobs, one as a day-care worker and three in nursing homes. Consistent with Stack's (1974) findings, Benita consistently maintained a positive relationship with all of her neighbors. They initially looked after her children when Benita spent a few days in jail because she was unable to pay off her accumulated traffic fines. Her next-door neighbor even transported all of her children to a relative's house while Benita strategized to raise the funds for her release.

Benita believed that she would be stranded without these vital relationships with friends and family. After her arrest, she received money from her children's father, her sister, and a neighbor she had known for a short time. She even accepted help from a former lover, a drug dealer whom she had broken up with because she did not want him around her children. She was grateful and appreciative but did not want to be indebted to them.

When I asked Benita whether she had ever been in love, she described the deep love and affection she still felt for Andre, the father of her two younger children. They were together five years but never married. She wanted to marry him because she was young and in love, but marriage did not fit Andre's lifestyle as a drug dealer (Miller 1995). But in retrospect, citing his criminal record and prison stints, she said she was very happy they did not marry.

After his release from prison, Andre ended up marrying an older woman. Both he and his wife, Alana, were very involved in the lives of his children with Benita (he had no other children). Andre's wife's earnings were his primary means of support. Benita sympathized with Andre, arguing that the amount of money he was required to pay in child support made it very difficult for him to afford housing and transportation. While his financial contributions were sporadic, she greatly appreciated the time he spent with all of her children. Even her two children from another man recognized Andre as their father.

Policy Changes and Consequences

Since the late 1990s, the emergence of a lower-paying, service-oriented economy for less-skilled workers, in addition to welfare reform and rising rates of incarceration among poor black men, has challenged the fragile networks on which impoverished black women such as Benita had previously relied. In *All Our Kin* (1974), Carol Stack described networks that mothers formed within their neighborhoods based mostly on their own relatives and, depending on the circumstances, the families of their children's fathers. Today, such networks are increasingly under threat. While mothers, sisters, aunts, and grandmothers continue to be valuable sources of support, they are not dependably so. Many women are feeling the pressures of limited personal resources and the economic marginalization of other family members, especially black men.

Stack conducted her study in the late 1960s, when Aid to Families with Dependent Children (AFDC) allowed a woman to stay at home with preschool-age children. In contrast, Benita lived under the regime imposed by Temporary Assistance to Needy Families (TANF), the welfare-reformed AFDC, which limits cash payments, puts a five-year lifetime maximum on receipt of services, and imposes training and work requirements. TANF aims to reduce "dependency" on public services by promoting job preparation, work, and marriage; to prevent pregnancies among unmarried women; and to encourage the formation and maintenance of two-parent families (U.S. Department of Health and Human Services 2011).

Required job-training programs placed many women in jobs in health care that don't pay enough to support themselves or their families. For example, although Benita benefited from her initial vocational training as a nurse's aide, she said:

> I think welfare reform is a joke. . . . After going through their twelve-week nursing program, you expect me to go out here and jump at a job working almost thirty hours mandatory a week, no babysitter, no dependable transportation, and seven to eight dollars an hour with no benefits? I mean, let's be real; my thing is if you [are] going to give me something that I can use, make it a real tool.

Accordingly, Benita was able to find work as a nurse's aide in senior centers, but her family responsibilities made it difficult for her to keep her job. To compensate for her fragile kin networks, Benita utilized services available through a neighborhood church that provided after-school tutoring and meals. Although she described herself as religious, she rarely attended church services because she felt uncomfortable about the congregation's familiarity with her financial struggles.

During the past fifteen years, a set of substantial public policy changes has exacerbated the difficulties of the poor. These "reforms," made by politicians who are far removed from the lives of low-income families, have shaped and reshaped the coping strategies they adopt and the social networks upon which they rely. In Bristol Hill, key policy shifts include the proliferation of state, county, and city police patrols; the closure of two public schools and opening of two charter schools; and the mass relocation of residents from a public housing project to this community.

In addition to the replacement of AFDC by TANF, the Quality Housing and Work Responsibility Act of 1998 aimed to reduce the concentration of poverty and move public housing residents into mixed-income private housing through the Section 8 voucher program. Benita had been on the list for public/subsidized housing for two years. When I spoke to a housing official concerning the long waiting list, I was told that the public housing units were overcrowded and that problem had to be dealt with before anyone on the waiting list could be accommodated. While changes in federal housing policy helped poor families find affordable housing outside of publicly owned, concentrated projects and TANF moved some women from welfare to work, both involved substantial disruptions in the lives of poor families.

If we consider these changes in public welfare and housing policy in conjunction with changes in the criminal justice system, we see that poor people confined in the nation's segregated ghettos have been negatively and disproportionately affected. The number of people in prison increased substantially after the imposition of mandatory sentencing for violations of drug laws. By 2001, 16.6 percent of all African American males were or had previously been incarcerated; the chance of an African American male going to prison was one in three (Bonczar 2003; Wildeman 2009; Pettit and Western 2004; Western and Beckett 1999; Bureau of Justice Statistics 2003). With regard to the two fathers of Benita's children, incarceration created an additional burden on both her parenting and her financial resources. The combined effects of her children's fathers' incarceration, her unstable housing situation, and her low wages were evident in Benita's everyday life.

Bristol Hill has felt the effects of policy changes in other areas as well, including policing and education. The robust drug trade has prompted a heavy police presence, leading to patrols and arrests by local, county, state, and federal law enforcement agencies. Yet intensive policing has failed to reduce the availability of drugs, and since the 1980s the neighborhood has suffered from disproportionate police activity with little benefit to anyone. Police contact occurs in the home as well as on the street, and most residents interact with law enforcement in some way, from neighborhood patrols to calling the police to report a crime. The neighborhood also faces serious educational problems. In recent years, the Bristol Hill school system has had the worst academic performance in the state. The state took over the public schools, established two K–8 charter schools, and placed the only high school in the hands of a private corporation. A year later, one elementary school and one middle school were closed. In Benita's case, the state takeover of the neighborhood schools meant that her children attended different schools even though they were close in age. Evictions, strained finances, poor-quality learning opportunities, and arrests are nothing new to low-income families; what is new is the disproportionate concentration of these "reform" policies on poor people and their cumulative impact on family stability.

Common Strategies for Coping with Poverty

The practices Benita adopted for coping with poverty are widely shared in her community, and her story offers a detailed picture of the survival strategies of poor black women across the country (Presser 1980; Rainwater 1970). Families like Benita's were first described by Joyce Ladner in *Tomorrow's Tomorrow* (1971) and Carol Stack's *All Our Kin* (1974), which focused on the strategies and practices young African American girls used in the face of poverty. Ladner's work influenced Stack's critique of the prevalent theory of "the culture of poverty."

Countering the allegations made in the infamous Moynihan Report (1965), Stack argued that poverty is not a self-perpetuating "cycle" that results from a "tangle of pathology" in black families. Rather, the lack of employment, a living wage, and affordable housing force people to behave in alternative ways to ensure their children's survival and success. Poverty is not the result of personal failings or cultural defects but of economic deprivation, she maintained. Chronic unemployment and underemployment; insecure, low-wage jobs; and crowded living quarters are simply conditions of poverty (Stack 1974, 23).

Challenging conventional thinking, Stack uncovered the networks of relatives and fictive kin that make female-headed black families resilient despite their limited resources. Stack argued that middle-class norms, such as households with male breadwinners and female homemakers, can be realized only with sufficient economic opportunity, which does not exist in black inner-city neighborhoods. Her contention that poor inner-city families and communities are not "disorganized" but instead pursue survival strategies that make sense in their own social context remains relevant for understanding how poor families manage today.

Elijah Anderson developed a strain theory based on his ethnographic work in Philadelphia to help explain what happens when kinship and friendship networks are stressed by deepening impoverishment. Anderson examines the interactions and negotiations for resources among the poor that shape life in increasingly isolated inner-city neighborhoods (Anderson 1990, 2000, 2008). According to Anderson, the ghetto economy at "ground zero" rests on three prongs: low-wage jobs that offer little continuity of employment and few benefits; welfare payments, including TANF, food stamps, and housing subsidies; and the informal economy. The informal sector encompasses legal activities carried on outside the marketplace, such as bartering goods and services among friends and relatives; semi-legal activities such as small, unregulated businesses operated out of the home; and illegal activities such as drug dealing, prostitution, and street crime (Anderson 2008, 8). As Anderson points out, drastic reductions in welfare payments and the contraction of job opportunities for less-educated workers mean that more inner-city residents must turn to informal economic activities, or "hustles," to get by.

Benita's account is an excellent example of Anderson's strain theory; the lack of resources among all those who share this situation generates tensions, and even ruptures, in their relationships. But that is only part of the story; how she navigated this terrain is even more telling. While most of these crises were precipitated by events that were out of her control, Benita took personal responsibility for her failings, as well as the failings of those around her. Our focus here is understanding how the crises unfold and are eventually resolved. Her interpretation of these events is significant; she took ownership of her situations.

From this viewpoint, her low wages were a result of her lack of education. She identified her problems—insufficient pay, high rents, poor-quality schools, and traffic tickets—as being unfair, but she attributed her predicament to her own actions rather than to the slumlords, health-care companies, or law enforcement officers. Her personal troubles were all her own, and although she pointed out that her story was the story of other women in Bristol Hill, it ended there.

The lack of affordable housing, teen pregnancy, low wages, police stops, poor schools, and incarceration were not problems Benita recognized explicitly as conditions produced by outside forces. Instead, she attributed many of her troubles to the failure of her parents and her own failure to acquire a better education. She saw her situation in very individualistic terms and, surprisingly, made no judgment on the fairness or equity of the system itself. In this respect, she adopted a conventional middle-class attitude.

When I asked her to reflect on her circumstances, Benita attributed her traffic tickets to her driving without insurance, although she could not afford either; her low wages to her lack of a college degree, rather than to her difficulties with child care; her teenage pregnancy and dropping out of high school to her mother's failure to prevent her from having sex, as well as not forcing her to go to school; and her eviction cycle to her inability to get into public housing, although she was aware that housing was overpriced and that slumlords need the upfront payment of first and last months' rent and security deposit to make a profit.

Here is where practices and accounts differ. When I asked her why she participated in my study, Benita said her sense-making was localized to herself and those around her, not generalized to an unfair opportunity structure. Even with the best of attitudes, she knew one thing for certain: given her resources, a new crisis was always on the horizon.

Stack (1974) proposed that public policies be configured with an understanding of the social practices and everyday lives of those who are most deeply affected by them. This study responds to that challenge by examining the intersections of policies affecting the poor and what happens to familial and fictive kinship, lovers and companions, and friendship networks when the resources available to them are drastically reduced. The practices that I examine should be understood in context as a set of strategies oriented toward the exigencies of this particular place and time. These policy reforms, however, have similar consequences for inner-city families nationally.

Analyzing the interactional order of Bristol Hill, I have examined how Benita performed her multiple roles given her circumstances; what strategies she used and how she learned them; how she was rewarded and sanctioned; how others recognized or made sense of her; how she managed at the home and in the workplace; and how her circumstances changed over time. By situating Benita's story in its cultural, historical, and social contexts, we can see how her life was affected by welfare reform, housing reform, education reform, and the war on drugs.

Reflections on Making Choices and Taking Responsibility

During my second year in the field, Benita asked me what I would do if I were in her shoes. "I don't know," I responded. "I haven't really thought about it." Two years later, she posed the same question to me: "If you were raising a family here, what would you do?" I tried to defer and said, "I don't know; I'm not a parent." "Bullshit," she responded. "You've thought about it." "Well," I replied, "given the state of the schools, the drug trade, the violence, the job prospects, the low wages, and the quality of housing, I would probably try to find a better place to live." "I am not going anywhere," she responded. "I can't go anywhere right now; there's just too much going on to even think about moving. The problems I have are gonna be my problems no matter where I go." After a brief moment of silence, I looked her in the eye and said, smiling, "Things change, and nobody knows the future."

I was telling her, in essence, to move away from Bristol Hill and find better opportunities elsewhere. Yet I had sought to learn from her and understand her strategies for survival, because her personal troubles and her experiences in relation to her broader community shed light on wider issues situated in this space (on personal troubles versus public issues, see Mills 2000). I was bothered by my response, however. I had never contemplated a fundamental question: what if she didn't want to leave Bristol Hill?

What options do families have when unemployment is unusually high, when schools are not performing, when neighborhoods are overrun with crime, when law enforcement does not consistently respond, and when a third of the children live in poverty? What is to be done? I identified a number of other problems that interested me as a sociologist, as well as problems Benita identified as a participant, which included various poorly functioning institutions.

The assumption was that if she remained, her children would likely receive a poor education while living in a dangerous space with few, if any, job prospects. Yet I came to realize that if I lived in this community, I would do what other parents have had to do: figure out strategies to secure a quality education, avoid criminal networks, and constantly monitor and advocate for my child. In my initial question to Benita, I failed to acknowledge simple realities such as the cost of moving, the price of housing, and the importance of social networks including family, schools, physicians, friends, and religious institutions. Moreover, I did not factor in the optimistic view that someday things might get better.

The methods Benita used to manage her life, given her limited resources, provide a glimpse into the level of sophistication and strategic ability required to navigate her world. In essence, Benita managed a constant state of crisis. Benita demonstrates what skills are required to survive the recurring crises that are endemic to concentrated poverty.

Benita's story shows that several of Stack's major points about poverty remain relevant today. For Stack's central character, Ruby Banks, "making it" included swapping and sharing resources. For Benita and women like her, every friend and family member must be looked at as a potential resource. The possibility of becoming homeless and having her children taken away was an uncomfortable reality that she dealt with daily. The high rate of incarceration for black fathers; the rising costs of food, housing, and energy; the limitations imposed by government austerity measures; a service sector that depends on low wages and unstable jobs; limited adult supervision for children; and overextended social networks have all made the lives of the poor even more challenging. Fortunately, familial networks appear to be durable and forgiving; the passing of time and impending crises repair familial breaches, as do occasions for celebration.

To a careful observer, it is obvious that Benita is constantly anticipating the next crisis that her circumstances are likely to precipitate. While her troubles with housing, job training, low wages, the police, and teen pregnancy seemed to me to be clearly related to wider societal issues, Benita saw these problems as temporary and the result of her personal failure. While visible class and racial disparities abound within her community, the constant effort to manage multiple crises seemed to render them tangential. Her optimism was embedded in her ability to manage as best she could, "making it" by any means necessary.

Anderson's model of the three-pronged ghetto economy illustrates the predicaments of people living in impoverished inner-city communities, but their coping strategies shed more light on how they survive, and even thrive. Benita used the local culture to make sense of her situation, and she exploited every opportunity to reconcile the discrepancy between the resources she needed and the limited and sporadic availability of opportunities to acquire them. Benita had to work at jobs that did not pay a living wage, use deceptive tactics to maintain housing and get to work, ritualistically go through the motions required by welfare reform, and sign up for public housing while knowing that these programs would ultimately fail her family. Above all, she tried to keep her children from repeating her mistakes.

Her circumstances are neither isolated nor unique. Problems of insufficient education, the lack of affordable housing, and low wages affect most poor families. Without intervention and a reexamination of the synergistic effects of separately conceived policies on poor families, many will continue to be placed in dire straits. Looking at this situation through the lens of an interaction order of poverty management shows how practices of law enforcement, employment, and job training impose requirements and expectations that make impoverished families more susceptible to disruption. Using an interaction-order approach to understand poor people's sensemaking and coping strategies is crucial if we are to better serve their good-faith efforts at self-sufficiency.

During our last interview, I asked Benita how she saw herself. She responded:

I see myself as somebody having the potential to be, you know, I can be whatever I wanted to be. I just don't have the tools to get over that barrier to, you know, even attempt to try to go on. . . . I don't have the tools in front of me. But I mean, I'm a beautiful person, I work well with people, I'm caring, and me doing the job that I'm doing, I wanna continue to do that, but I wanna push further to, you know, be more at what I'm doing. 'Cause, like, right now, nine dollars an hour? I know so much stuff. I don't have the tools to go on to college right now. . . . It's too much stuff going on. There's no way that I could possibly do that right now. So now I have to try to figure out a way to do that, just to do better and be better.

Understanding Everyday Life in the Shadow of Poverty and Drug Dealing

This ethnography of Lyford Street illuminates the complexities of concentrated poverty. The people who live in this neighborhood share these difficult experiences, and because of the fragility of their common predicament they take a nonjudgmental approach to others who find themselves in precarious situations. The problems of Bristol Hill residents arise from the absence of resource-rich networks, their exclusion by reasons of race and class from equal educational and employment opportunities, the lack of meaningful interactions with those in positions of authority, and policies that impose sanctions that cumulatively become a form of collective punishment (Rios 2011; Laub and Sampson 2003). These problems are being played out on a larger scale all over the world as global capitalism diminishes public concern for those who are caught in concentrated poverty. Focusing on residents' attempts to cope with their predicament shows how dominant social institutions lead to mass incarceration and create a system of collective punishment. The people who live there understand the social problems that afflict their community. Only they know what measures would assist them in fulfilling their goals to live decent lives—if policy makers would ask them and grant them a substantial role in designing and administering the solutions. The resourcefulness and creativity of those struggling just to get by could reshape these neighborhoods while extending the reciprocity that exists within this community to their relationship with the dominant society (Lareau 2003).

The interaction order on Lyford Street is centered on reciprocities in action, not on abstract values. The system does not work unless residents make a mutual commitment to one another, especially when they know the rules by which they must play are unfair. Residents of the neighborhood closely tie their practices and sense-making to the fairness that exists within this neighborhood for themselves, one another, and especially their children.

This ethnographic approach has provided a deeper understanding of how residents navigate, conform to, and resist the local social order. In order to make sense of life on Lyford Street, we must comprehend the layout of the neighborhood, the various social actors and groups involved, and the functioning of the drug trade, as well as the instability of the economy. Few people outside communities like Bristol Hill, which are found throughout the country, can imagine the social order and high degree of organization that exist there. Although some social theorists suggest that the major problems of black ghettos lie in their isolation from mainstream society, the reverse is true: people who live in Bristol Hill are well aware of how the rest of the world works, but those who make decisions for the people who live in Bristol Hill have little or no meaningful interaction with its residents. The distance between insiders and outsiders generates tension and misunderstanding in face-to-face interactions. The men and women who told me their stories find it difficult at best, and at worst impossible, to fulfill the outsiders' expectations. Their lives are under constant scrutiny by the state, and that surveillance leads almost invariably to arrests, fines, and incarceration. Other sanctions enforced by landlords and potential employers penetrate all aspects of life, exacerbating the precarious nature of everyday existence in poverty.

An interaction-order approach not only offers a different way of understanding these communities but also aids in resolving contested questions about culture, social disorganization, and collective efficacy. Everyone must respond to the local interaction order. The contingencies of *this* place, as in all places, are managed by enacting identities and performing practices that are consistent with them. Without meaningful interactions between local residents and those who control resources or occupy positions of power and make life-altering choices for this community, the roots of the poverty that afflicts Bristol Hill and places like it will remain misunderstood, and solutions will be based on statistical correlations rather than on an understanding of the interaction patterns that provide a modicum of predictability in everyday life. Many of the strategies that are practiced on Lyford Street are shaped by constraints imposed by the setting even as they aim to meet the expectations of the outside world. Yet they work not because such efforts are rewarded—indeed, they are often heavily sanctioned—but because people who live in this neighborhood realize that they can rely only on one another.

In order to understand how outsiders' sense-making differs from that of insiders, I interrogated the role of information with regard to gossip versus snitching, the politics of murder, and the harm that comes from treating particular human lives differently. Through the narratives of people such as Benita, Mr. John, Mrs. Wells, Brent, Usman, Dave, and Fred, I have shown the tensions that arise when residents attempt to conform to both internal and external expectations: when policies fail to take local dynamics into account, they set people up for failure. For those with few legal ways of earning a living, the opportunities offered by the underground economy are inescapable. The view that residents and drug dealers are separate groups with conflicting interests assumes that this community would be better off if all these young men were in jail. By all accounts, however, this neighborhood and others like it have become worse off as young men are prevented from acting as partners in parenting. The commonsense world of Lyford Street is organized by rules of reciprocity and trust based on shared understandings. Comprehending the premises that underlie common practices offers a different perspective on Jonathan's involvement in the drug trade and on the interaction order of the community as a whole. Residents of Bristol Hill are not merely victims of their circumstances; they are active agents, and their survival is dependent upon how they treat and understand one another.

Outsiders tend to scrutinize individuals and their conduct instead of reexamining the public policies that generate their predicaments. The taken-for-granted assumptions of outside policy makers are called into question when we see that it is impossible for people to fulfill their own aspirations, let alone public officials' expectations. The lives of the men and women in this book involve elaborate survival strategies that shift from moment to moment but never enable them to attain a modicum of security. Inability to pay your debts or adequately monitor your children, unreliable and often punitive policing, and being confined to an unstable, low-wage job market all limit opportunities. Another component of the misalignment between outsider and insider expectations is apparent in how society encourages and enforces conformity through sanctions.

Outsiders contend that many people grow up in similar circumstances without committing a crime involving the sale or use of drugs or being associated with violence. This argument suggests that those who become involved have better options available to them that they inexplicably fail to choose. But it is almost impossible for anyone on Lyford Street to avoid participating in the local social order; indeed, it would be foolhardy to try. As Mr. John explained, "I don't use drugs or sell them, but I'm in the world with them." The limited resources and lack of alternatives available in the neighborhood strengthen residents' reliance on one another. Drug dealing is just one of many problems that must be factored into the interaction order

of Lyford Street. Focusing on values and beliefs in an effort to explain concentrated poverty is wrongheaded; the conviction that the poor are responsible for their own position reinforces and sanctifies the status quo.

The lenient attitude of members of the community toward drug dealing and their willingness to benefit from its profits make sense to insiders
and those who are familiar with daily life in this neighborhood. Residents'
strength of commitment to and level of participation in the drug trade rest
on their limited job opportunities, inadequate educational programs, low
property values, nonexistent savings, and a lack of public safety, all leading
to deep financial and personal stress. While boys' involvement may arise
from proximity to and familiarity with the local order of drug dealing, men's
careers are shaped by their inability to secure a livelihood through legal
means. If we look at Jonathan's lack of knowledge about the job market,
Dave's account of selling drugs to compensate for his low wages, and Benita's
risking jail just to drive to work every day, we gain a more nuanced view of
personal responsibility and the work ethic. Moreover, the high probability
that neighborhood youths will carry arrest records into adulthood substantially diminishes their employment prospects. Being able to obtain conventional social markers of sustainable wages, independent housing, and
starting a family gives people hope, which is a precondition for not simply
surviving in the here and now but planning for a future.

A recognition of the mutually reinforcing obstacles faced by people living in concentrated poverty is key to understanding the strategies they em-
ploy. The situation on Lyford Street is symptomatic of the continued decline
of inner-city neighborhoods, and its residents are among the innumerable
U.S. citizens who face long-term poverty, intractable debt, probable incarceration, and a considerably shortened life expectancy. The consequences
are especially dire for those who aspire to become self-sufficient but lack
the tools and opportunities to do so. Deindustrialization and the shift to a
service-oriented economy that does not pay a living wage to those without
advanced educational qualifications has left very few options for the urban
poor. In an environment in which success can seldom be achieved through
legitimate means, people seek out alternative approaches. The imperative of
survival may push men and women toward strategies that mean the difference between life and death, not only for themselves but for their children.

This study has explored how residents of a poor neighborhood navigate
a world in which the scant resources that existed in the past—industrial
jobs for workers without technical skills, public housing for working-class
families, and a safety net for the children of single mothers—have either
vanished or been deliberately abolished. People must constantly improvise

livelihoods for themselves and others who depend on them. The sanctions tied to services urgently needed by the poor not only exacerbate their deprivation but also create a system of collective punishment. Unrealistic child-support payments, extortionate fines and even jail stays for minor traffic violations, debts that pile up when people toil at jobs that do not pay a living wage and inhabit housing that is not affordable—all trap people in poverty as surely as others' attempts to earn money by drug dealing lead to their incarceration.

Coping with poverty requires a set of skills that are informed by direct experiences of living with failing schools, under- and unemployment, mass incarceration, and an embedded drug trade in their community. But the very practices needed for survival with limited resources are treated as deviant. For those under the most social and economic strain, conforming to overlapping but incompatible policies becomes deviant as well. Benita dealt with tickets for driving to work, evictions due to her inability to pay rent, and a welfare policy that expected her to be a full-time parent and worker simultaneously. Women like Benita do not complain about their inadequate wages and unstable jobs, why the fathers of their children enter the drug trade, or why so many men and women end up in prison or suffer an untimely death. Benita takes personal responsibility for her choices, as do most of those I interviewed. Yet everyone knows that something is amiss. When a resident was illegally evicted, he was hesitant to call the police because he knew that they would find fault with him rather than his landlord. Many people who live on Lyford Street do not seek recourse from basic social institutions, especially the police, because whenever they do, they end up worse off.

The problems that beset a small city like Bristol Hill, whose social fabric is knit together by strong family and friendship ties, could be solved, but effective remedies would require long-term, sustainable commitments that privilege insiders. Underlying this community's chronic impoverishment are structural factors, especially the limited availability of economic opportunities for black men, but this chronic poverty has been deepened by gravely misconceived social policies devised by outsiders. Those who have resources have deliberately segregated themselves from the poor. Inequality and social distance profoundly distort the power dynamics between those who make policy and those who are subject to it. The lack of reciprocity and the absence of meaningful interactions between the architects of social welfare programs and those whom they are supposed to serve leads to misguided policies with regard to employment, housing, and criminal justice.

BIBLIOGRAPHY

Adler, Patricia A. 1993. *Wheeling and dealing: An ethnography of an upper-level drug dealing and smuggling community.* New York: Columbia University Press.

Adler, Patricia A., and Peter Adler. 1983. Shifts and oscillations in deviant careers: The case of upper-level drug dealers and smugglers. *Social Problems* 31:195–207.

Anderson, Elijah. 1990. *Streetwise: Race, class, and change in an urban community.* Chicago: University of Chicago Press.

———. 2000. *The code of the street: Decency, violence, and the moral life of the inner city.* New York: W.W. Norton.

———. 2003. *A place on the corner.* University of Chicago Press.

Anderson, Elijah, ed. 2008. *Against the wall: Poor, young, black, and male.* Philadelphia: University of Pennsylvania Press.

Becker, Howard S. 1973. *Outsiders: Studies in the sociology of deviance.* New York: Free Press.

Black, Timothy. 2009. *When a heart turns rock solid: The lives of three Puerto Rican brothers on and off the streets.* New York: Pantheon.

Bonczar, Thomas. 2003. *The prevalence of imprisonment in the U.S. population, 1974–2004.* Washington, DC: U.S. Department of Justice, Bureau of Justice Statistics.

Bourgois, Philippe. 1995. *In search of respect: Selling crack in El Barrio.* Cambridge: Cambridge University Press.

Bureau of Justice Statistics. 2003. Prevalence of imprisonment in the United States 1974–2001. http://www.ojp.usdoj.gov/bjs/pub/pdf/piusp01.pdf

Clear, Todd R. 2007. *Imprisoning communities: How mass incarceration makes disadvantaged neighborhoods worse.* New York: Oxford University Press.

Collins, Jane L., and Victoria Mayer. 2010. *Both hands tied: Welfare reform and the race to the bottom in the low-wage labor market.* Chicago: University of Chicago Press.

Collins, Randall. 2009. *Violence: A micro-sociological theory.* Santa Barbara: Greenwood Publishing Group.

Contreras, Randol. 2012. *The stickup kids: Race, drugs, violence, and the American dream.* Berkeley: University of California Press.

Desmond, Matthew. 2012a. Eviction and the reproduction of urban poverty. *American Journal of Sociology* 118 (1): 88–133.

———. 2012b. Disposable ties and the urban poor. *American Journal of Sociology* 117 (5): 1295–1335.

Duck, Waverly. 2009. Black male sexual politics: Avoidance of HIV/AIDS testing as a masculine health practice. *Journal of African American Studies* 13:283–306.

Duck, Waverly, and Anne Rawls. 2012. Interaction orders of drug dealing spaces: Local orders of sensemaking in a poor Black American place. *Crime, Law and Social Change* 57 (1): 33–75.

Fader, Jamie J. 2013. *Falling back: Incarceration and transitions to adulthood among urban youth*. New Brunswick, NJ: Rutgers University Press.

Fine, Gary Alan. 2003. Towards a peopled ethnography developing theory from group life. *Ethnography* 4:41–60.

Garfinkel, Harold. 1963. A conception of and experiments with "trust" as a condition of stable concerted actions. In *Motivation and social interaction*, edited by O. J. Harvey, 187–238. New York: Ronald Press.

———. 1967. *Studies in ethnomethodology*. Englewood Cliffs, NJ: Prentice Hall.

———. 2006. *Seeing sociologically: The routine grounds of social action*. Boulder, CO: Paradigm.

Garfinkel, Harold, and Anne Warfield Rawls. 2008. *Toward a sociological theory of information*. Boulder, CO: Paradigm.

Garot, Robert J. 2007. "Where you from!" Gang identity as performance. *Journal of Contemporary Ethnography* 36 (1): 50–84.

Goffman, Alice. 2014. *On the run: Fugitive life in an American city*. Chicago: University of Chicago Press.

Goffman, Erving. 1959. *The presentation of self in everyday life*. New York: Doubleday/Anchor.

———. 1983. Presidential address: The interaction order. *American Sociological Review* 48:1–17.

Gould, Roger V. 2003. *Collision of wills: How ambiguity about social rank breeds conflict*. Chicago: University of Chicago Press.

Hamer, Jennifer. 2001. *What it means to be Daddy: Fatherhood for black men living away from their children*. New York: Columbia University Press.

Harding, David J. 2010. *Living the drama: Community, conflict, and culture among inner-city boys*. Chicago: University of Chicago Press.

Holzer, Harry J., Paul Offner, and Elaine Sorensen. 2005. Declining employment among young black less-educated men: The role of incarceration and child support. *Journal of Policy Analysis and Management* 24 (2): 329–50.

Holzer, Harry J., and Jess Reaser. 2000. Black applicants, black employees, and urban labor market policy. *Journal of Urban Economics* 48 (3): 365–87.

Horowitz, Ruth. 1983. *Honor and the American dream: Culture and identity in a Chicano community*. New Brunswick, NJ: Rutgers University Press.

Jacobs, Bruce A. 1999. Crack to heroin? Drug markets and transition. *British Journal of Criminology* 39:555–74.

———. 2004. A typology of street criminal retaliation. *Journal of Research in Crime and Delinquency* 41:295–323.

Jacobs, Bruce A., Volkan Topalli, and Richard Wright. 2003. Carjacking, street life, and offender motivation. *British Journal of Criminology* 43:673–88.

Jacobs, Bruce A., and Richard Wright. 2006. *Street justice: Retaliation in the criminal underworld*. New York: Cambridge University Press.

Katz, Jack. 2008. *Seductions of crime: Moral and sensual attractions in doing evil*. New York: Basic Books.

Ladner, Joyce A. 1971. *Tomorrow's tomorrow: The black woman*. Garden City, NY: Doubleday.

Lareau, Annette. 2003. *Unequal childhoods: Class, race, and family life.* Berkeley: University of California Press.

Laub, John H., and Leana C. Allen. 2000. Life course criminology and community corrections. *Perspectives* 24:20–29.

Laub, John H., and Robert J. Sampson. 1995. The long-term effects of punitive discipline. In *Coercion and punishment in long-term perspectives,* edited by Joan McCord, 247–58. Cambridge: Cambridge University Press.

———. 1998. The long-term reach of adolescent competence: Socioeconomic achievement in the lives of disadvantaged men. In *Competence and character through life,* edited by Anne Colby, Jacquelyn James, and Daniel Hart, 89–112. Chicago: University of Chicago Press.

———. 2001. Understanding desistance from crime. In *Crime and justice: A review of research,* vol. 28, edited by Michael Tonry, 1–69. Chicago: University of Chicago Press.

———. 2003. *Shared beginnings, divergent lives: Delinquent boys to age 70.* Cambridge, MA: Harvard University Press.

Liebow, Elliot. 1967. *Tally's corner: A study of streetcorner men.* Boston: Little, Brown.

Lewis, Oscar. 1961. *Children of Sanchez: Autobiography of a Mexican family.* New York: Vintage.

MacLeod, Jay. 1987. *Ain't no makin' it: Aspirations and attainment in a low income neighborhood.* Boulder, CO: Westview.

Maher, Lisa. 1997. *Sexed work: Gender, race, and resistance in a Brooklyn drug market.* Oxford: Oxford University Press.

Manning, Peter K. 1977. *Police work: The social organization of policing.* Cambridge, MA: MIT Press.

———. 1980. *The narcs' game: Organizational and informational limits on drug law enforcement.* Cambridge, MA: MIT Press.

———. 2008. *The technology of policing: Crime mapping, information technology and the rationality of crime control.* New York: New York University Press.

Massey, Douglas S., and Nancy A. Denton. 1993. *American apartheid: Segregation and the making of the underclass.* Cambridge, MA: Harvard University Press.

Matza, David. 1964. *Delinquency and drift.* New York: John Wiley and Sons.

Mayer, Susan. 1997. *What money can't buy: Family income and children's life chances.* Cambridge, MA: Harvard University Press.

Miller, Jody. 1995. Gender and power in the streets. *Journal of Contemporary Ethnography* 23:427–52.

Mills, C. Wright. 2000. *The sociological imagination.* New York: Oxford University Press.

Moore, Joan W. 1985. Isolation and stigmatization in the development of an underclass: The case of Chicano gangs in East Los Angeles. *Social Problems* 33 (1): 1–12.

Moore, Joan W., Robert Garcia, and Carlos Garcia. 1978. *Homeboys: Gangs, drugs, and prison in the barrios of Los Angeles.* Philadelphia: Temple University Press

Morenoff, Jeffrey, Robert J. Sampson, and Stephen Raudenbush. 2001. Neighborhood inequality, collective efficacy, and the spatial dynamics of urban violence. *Criminology* 39:517–60.

Moskos, Peter. 2008. *Cop in the hood: My year policing Baltimore's eastern district.* Princeton, NJ: Princeton University Press.

Moynihan, Daniel P. 1965. *The Negro family: The case for national action.* Washington, DC: Office of Policy Planning and Research, U.S. Department of Labor.

Murphy, Sheigla, Dan Waldorf, and Craig Reinarman. 1990. Drifting into dealing: Becoming a cocaine seller. *Qualitative Sociology* 13 (4): 321–43.

Newman, Katherine S. 2000. *No shame in my game: The working poor in the inner city.* New York: Vintage.

Pager, Devah. 2008. *Marked: Race, crime, and finding work in an era of mass incarceration.* Chicago: University of Chicago Press.

Pate, David, and E. Johnson. 2000. The ethnographic study for the W-2 child support demonstration evaluation: Some preliminary findings. *Focus* 21 (1): 18–22.

Pattillo, Mary. 2007. *Black on the block: Politics of race and class in the city.* Chicago: University of Chicago Press.

Pattillo-McCoy, Mary. 1999. *Black picket fences: Privilege and peril among the black middle class.* Chicago: University of Chicago Press.

Pettit, Becky, and Bruce Western. 2004. Mass imprisonment and the life-course: Race and class inequality in U.S. incarceration. *American Sociological Review* 69:151–69.

Presser, Harriet B. 1980. Sally's corner: Coping with unmarried motherhood. *Journal of Social Issues* 36 (1): 107–29.

Presser, Lois. 2008. *Been a heavy life: Stories of violent men.* Urbana: University of Illinois Press.

Rainwater, Lee. 1970. *Behind ghetto walls: Black family life in a federal slum.* Piscataway, NJ: Aldine.

Rawls, Anne Warfield. 1987. The interaction order sui generis: Goffman's contribution to social theory. *Sociological Theory* 2:136–149.

———. 1998. Durkheim's challenge to philosophy: Human reason as a product of enacted social practice. *American Journal of Sociology* 3:887–901.

———. 2000. Race as an interaction order phenomenon: W. E. B. Du Bois's "double consciousness" thesis revisited. *Sociological Theory* 18:241–74.

———. 2009. An essay on two conceptions of social order constitutive orders of action, objects and identities vs. aggregated orders of individual action. *Journal of Classical Sociology* 9 (4): 500–20.

Rios, Victor, Jr. 2011. *Punished: Policing the lives of Black and Latino boys.* New York: New York University Press.

Rose, Dina R., and Todd R. Clear. 2004. Who doesn't know someone in jail? The impact of exposure to prison on attitudes toward formal and informal controls. *The Prison Journal* 84 (2): 228–47.

Rosenfeld, Richard, Bruce A. Jacobs, and Richard Wright. 2003. Snitching and the code of the streets. *British Journal of Criminology* 43:291–309.

Rosnow, Ralph L., and Gary Alan Fine. 1976. *Rumor and gossip: The social psychology of hearsay.* New York: Elsevier.

Sampson, Robert J. 2004. Neighborhood and community: Collective efficacy and community safety. *New Economy* 11:106–13.

Sampson, Robert J., and John H. Laub. 1990. Crime and deviance over the life course: The salience of adult social bonds. *American Sociological Review* 55:609–27.

———. 1992. Crime and deviance in the life course. *Annual Review of Sociology* 18:63–84.

Sharkey, Robert. 2013. *Stuck in place: Urban neighborhoods and the end of progress toward equality.* Chicago: University of Chicago Press.

Short, James F., Jr. 1974. Collective behavior, crime, and delinquency. *Handbook of criminology,* edited by D. Glasser, 403–49.

Small, Mario Luis, David J. Harding, and Michele Lamont. 2010. Reconsidering culture and poverty. *Annals of the American Academy of Political and Social Science* 629:6–27.

Sugrue, Thomas J. 2014. *The origins of the urban crisis: Race and inequality in postwar Detroit.* Princeton, NJ: Princeton University Press.

Stack, Carol. 1974. *All our kin: Strategies for survival in a black community.* New York: Harper & Row.

St. Jean, Peter K. B. 2008. *Pockets of crime: Broken windows, collective efficacy, and the criminal point of view.* Chicago: University of Chicago Press.

Suttles, Gerald D. 1968. *The social order of the slum.* Chicago: University of Chicago Press.

Thrasher, Frederic M. 1927. *The gang.* Chicago: University of Chicago Press.

Tyler, Tom R. 2004. Enhancing police legitimacy. *The Annals of the American Academy of Political and Social Science* 593 (1): 84–99.

U.S. Census Bureau. 2010. Population characteristics. www.census.gov

U.S. Department of Health and Human Services. 2011. Accessed November 12. http://www.acf.hhs.gov/programs/ofa/tanf/about.html.

Venkatesh, Sudhir. 1997. The social organization of street gang activity in an urban ghetto. *American Journal of Sociology* 103:82–111.

———. 2006. *Off the books: The underground economy of the urban poor.* Cambridge, MA: Harvard University Press.

Western, Bruce. 2002. The impact of incarceration on wage mobility and inequality. *American Sociological Review* 67 (4): 526–46.

Western, Bruce, and Katherine Beckett. 1999. How unregulated is the U.S. labor market? The penal system as a labor market institution. *American Journal of Sociology* 104 (4): 1030–60.

Western, Bruce, and Becky Pettit. 2000. Mass imprisonment and the life course: Race and class inequality in U.S. incarceration. *American Sociological Review* 69 (2):151–69.

Wieder, D. Lawrence. 1974. *Language and social reality: The case of telling the convict code.* The Hague: Mouton. Excerpt in *Ethnomethodology: Selected readings,* edited by Roy Turner, 144–72. Harmondsworth: Penguin.

Wildeman, Christopher. 2009. Parental imprisonment, the prison boom, and the concentration of childhood disadvantage. *Demography* 46:265–80.

Williams, Rhonda Y. 2005. *The politics of public housing: Black women's struggles against urban inequality.* New York: Oxford University Press.

Wilson, James Q., and George L. Kelling. 1982. The police and neighborhood safety: Broken windows. *Atlantic Monthly* 249:29–36, 38.

Wilson, William Julius. 1987. *The truly disadvantaged: The inner city, the underclass, and public policy.* Chicago: University of Chicago.

Woldoff, Rachael A. 2011. *White flight/black flight: The dynamics of racial change in an American neighborhood.* Ithaca, NY: Cornell University Press.

Yablonsky, Lewis. 1959. The delinquent gang as a near-group. *Social Problems* 7:108–17.

Young, Alford A. 2006. *The minds of marginalized black men: Making sense of mobility, opportunity, and future life chances.* Princeton, NJ: Princeton University Press.

INDEX